How to pass the
EMPLOYMENT INTERVIEW
(with flying colors)

How to pass the EMPLOYMENT INTERVIEW

(with flying colors)

W. G. RYCKMAN

DOW JONES-IRWIN
Homewood, Illinois 60430

ISBN 0-87094-291-3

Library of Congress Catalog Card No. 82-70157

Printed in the United States of America

1 2 3 4 5 6 7 8 9 0 K 9 8 7 6 5 4 3 2

Preface

This book is about that fine old art of surviving a job interview. It is probably most useful for young jobholders and persons about to be graduated from college or graduate school. But no matter who you are, this book will assist you in preparing for, and successfully surviving, the time-honored trial by fire: the job interview.

Each year a million and a quarter men and women graduate with a bachelor's or master's degree. In late winter and early spring thousands of recruiters descend on campuses across the land, dangling luscious job-offer plums from their fingers. There ensues a ritual as stylized and inflexible as the mating dance of the wandering albatross (*Diomedia exulans*) in the rocky wastes of Tristan da Cunha. Ornithologists tell us the female of the species lays but a single egg after mating. In contrast, the average job hunter, regardless of sex, lays a generous clutch of eggs—and accomplishes that feat prior to finding a mate. To mix the metaphor still further, at least one golden egg can usually be found among the infertile ones.

The steps of the mating ritual between the job hunter and the potential employer are: preparation and submission of the résumé, first interviews, call-back interviews, and offers; and finally the climax of the rite is reached when a graduate and an employer mate. At appropriate intervals in the process letters are written and received, rejection notices (bullets) are sent and accepted with resignation, and telephone calls are made. It is a traumatic experience for the soon-to-be-graduated student. The recruiter, too, has his problems. After all, he may have three jobs to offer and dozens of qualified applicants to choose from.

Since a large percentage of jobs are obtained through the campus interview process, this book will give special attention to that avenue, but it will also cover other methods frequently used by graduates to secure a position they want.

Every year tens of thousands of young executives, for one reason or another, decide to move to fresher fields, and while still employed, they seek other jobs more suited to their talents. We will have words of advice for this worthy group of men and women.

Good luck to you. I hope you find what you are looking for—in the book as well as in the job market.

W. G. Ryckman

Contents

1

Preparation for the job hunter

When you apply for a job, you are a salesman. Whether you go through the recruiting process at your school, engage in a letter writing blizzard, answer ads, or use an employment agency, you are attempting to sell your services to the most desirable employer on the best terms you can secure.

To be successful a salesman must know all there is to be known about his product. He must be thoroughly familiar with its strengths and weaknesses, with the limits of its capacity, and with the settings in which it will function to its greatest effect.

Self-analysis

Thus, as a job hunter, you should begin your campaign with an exhaustive self-analysis. Are you a gregarious individual with a sparkling personality and an ability to converse easily with strangers? Do you mingle freely with all kinds of people, or do you spend your time with a couple of close

1

friends far from the madding crowd? Your answers will indicate whether you would be happier and more productive in a position where you will meet the public rather than in a position where you will do research or financial analysis in the solitude of your office.

Go a step farther. Does the role you have assumed up to now represent what you would like to be in the future? Can you prepare for a change in your attitudes by seeking a position that will encourage the development of new personality traits? Think about that before you decide what type of job you would like to secure.

Think also of your capabilities. In what courses did you excel during your school years? Are you a mathematical wizard, a hotshot chemist or physicist? Does economics or accounting turn you on? Have you a well-defined career objective, or are you drifting along with the tide, with no real awareness of where you are heading? If so, you had better reach some conclusions in this area before you hit the job market and start selling yourself.

Don't stop with an analysis of personal characteristics. Consider where you will find the best niche for yourself. Which industries are on the up? Which are mature and can expect little growth? Which should be avoided because their sales will decline in the future? Where do you want to work? East, west, north, south? In the hinterlands or in a major metropolitan area? Does private industry attract you, or would you be happier and more productive with a nonprofit organization or even a government agency? What specific employers are best suited to meet your needs?

This sounds like a major undertaking, and it is—make no mistake about that. But it is a necessary chore that you must complete before you, as a salesman, can sell your product successfully.

Take a scratch pad and start with a list of your competencies. What work have you been trained to do? What job experience have you had? What courses in college or graduate school interested you the most? In what areas did you excel? Analyze yourself. Work on it; it won't come easy.

Analysis of job preferences

Consider what kinds of companies or organizations you would prefer to work for. Which ones will give you the best chance of achieving your career goals? Individual companies have individual characteristics. No two are exactly alike. Large companies have many opportunities but may lose sight of individuals in the mass of employees. Smaller companies afford greater variety in jobs; if you worked for such a company, you would be more of a generalist, less of a specialist. Smaller companies, however, are often gobbled up by larger ones, and this usually results in wholesale staffing changes. Nepotism may be rampant in closely held corporations.

Next, start analyzing industries. Which have the best prospects? Energy production will be of major importance in the years to come. What opportunities exist in this field? Will atomic energy always be under fire? Will domestic automobile manufacturing beat back the foreign competition? Is the recreational equipment industry leveling off? Think before you apply for a job with a specific company. Don't box yourself into a no-win situation. Analyze the companies within an industry. Automobile manufacturers are not alike. Chemical companies are not equally successful, and they do not have similar prospects. Pick the most promising targets.

Remember this: Pay is usually commensurate with contribution to company sales and profit. The best jobs are the ones that influence sales and profits the most. That is why selling is a highly paid profession. In addition, when earnings depend to a large extent on the performance of the individual, the hard-charging tiger can write his own ticket. His paycheck depends on his own production and is not controlled by the success or failure of others. Contrast the potential of the salesman with that of the person whose efforts are difficult to convert into an entry on the profit and loss statement. Will that person's pay and prospects suffer because the corporation has difficulty in measuring his contribution? Selling offers many advantages to a graduate seeking an entry-level job with a corporation. Experience in meeting people and knowing how to speak articulately and convincingly will be assets no matter where an individual finds himself in the future.

Think also of your personality. Are you a take-charge person, strong on ambition, with high aspirations? Do you relish challenge and pressure? Do you want a fast track to promotion and financial independence? If so, you will not look for a job with a staid old company that plugs along at a moderate pace year after year. Such a company offers low risk and high security, but it provides few opportunities for advancement. On the other hand, working for a young, innovative, up-and-coming company in a new and growing industry will offer many personal advantages, but these will be accompanied by much greater risk and heavy pressure. Such jobs are not nine-to-five deals. Workweeks of 60 to 70 hours are not unusual, nor is weekend work. The return may be impressive, but so is the price for success. Moreover, the possibility is great that not all of the "up-and-coming" companies will be successful over the long run. Many may fall by the wayside.

Analysis of career goals

In short, what are your career goals? If you want to make a lot of money quickly, don't look for a job with a public utility or enter government service. Are you willing to pay the ante for the privilege of playing in a high-stakes game?

Nothing comes for free in this world, and you'd better believe it. Apartments on Park Avenue, condominiums in Palm Beach, fancy cars, and expensive tastes are great, but the money to pay for them doesn't grow on trees.

In 2O years' time a job somewhere in the Carolinas may pay only a third as much as a lucrative berth on Wall Street, but there is something to be said for being able to knock off Wednesday afternoon for a golf game and to have an hour on the tennis court every evening before dark.

Some people won't be happy until they get to be president of their companies; some place a higher value on other aspects of their lives. I guess it all depends on what your goals are. That's your decision to make, and you ought to start making it before you begin your job hunt. What you decide will influence what kind of job you will seek and what type of employer you will focus on in your interviews.

Don't get me wrong. I'm not in any way opposed to material success. I, too, would like to enjoy the amenities that are available to the chairman of the board or the president. My point is—be aware of what you are getting into before you leap.

Take a good look at the management of a company that interests you. What can you learn about the top executives? What is their past history—did they rise from the ranks, or were they enticed from competitors? What is their philosophy of management? Are they active and respected in their communities? Are they the type of people you would like to associate with?

Planning ahead

On your list, include everything you can think of along these lines. Refine the list, and work on it over a long period of time. You should start on this analysis no later than the fall of your final school year. College seniors should also consider whether to enter graduate school immediately, to work two or three years before enrolling in graduate school, or to start their work career directly after graduation. If you plan to go to graduate school at any time in the future, begin your screening process early so you will pick the right school to help you meet your objectives.

Don't leave everything for when you enter the recruiting marathon a few months before graduation. Plan ahead: be prepared for what you will face. The ancient Greek philosopher who said, "Know thyself," had it right. You can't sell your product until you are thoroughly familiar with it.

When your list reaches its final form, you should have an excellent awareness of what you are, what you want, and what you are best equipped to do. You will know where you prefer to work and what type of organization is most suitable for your talents. You will have decided on your career objectives as you see them now, being aware that as you mature, so will your goals. Finally, you will have researched and chosen at least a dozen potential employers that will afford you the best opportunity both to demonstrate your worth as an employee and to achieve your personal goals. The organizations you have chosen will be your prime targets when the recruiting season opens. Other organizations will be added as you become aware of them.

The screening interview

Not until you are satisfied with your list should you begin to plan your interviewing strategy. One of the most useful tools you will have is your résumé, and we'll spend considerable time discussing this important document in Chapter 6. Your résumé will give details of your education, your experience, your interests, your job desires, and your career plans. A good résumé will not get you a job, but a poor one will start you off with two strikes against you.

When you enter the interview room, your direct selling begins. Good salesmen are polite, respectful; they are self-possessed, assured, articulate, and comfortable when talking to others. They are confident because they know everything there is to be known about the product they are selling. Yet, they do not allow their confidence to make them arrogant or superior. Competent people don't get steamrollered into buying a product they neither need nor want.

The interviewer is a willing buyer. He has jobs to fill, and he is in the market to fill them with the best product he can buy in his price range. The candidate must prove that he or she is the most qualified person to fill the interviewer's need. He will utilize all the nuggets of wisdom scattered through these pages. He will handle himself immaculately, speak convincingly, have a reply for every question thrown at him, and come across as the type of person who would fit smoothly into an organization.

Very seldom does a job offer come at the end of a screening interview. At least one more meeting usually takes place, and many more issues, including salary, have to be settled before the deal is consummated. Nevertheless, the candidate should attempt to get a preliminary commitment from the recruiter at the end of the first interview. His objective is to make sure the door is left open for further discussion. To do this he should close the interview by saying something like the following: "Thank you for your time, Mr. Spencer. I am very interested in your company and the opportunity we have been discussing. How soon can I expect to hear from you?" The last sentence is the clincher. Try for a positive response, and lay the groundwork for a telephone call if you do not hear from the recruiter by the established date.

From this point on in your negotiations, try for a commitment to further action at the conclusion of every meeting, phone call, or letter. Try not to leave anything hanging in midair. Nail it down; make sure both sides understand what happens next.

Hints:

- ☐ Go into training for the interview season.
- ☐ Analyze your product. What is it, and what is the best use for it?
- ☐ Analyze your market. Where will your product find the best reception? To whom will it be most valuable?
- ☐ Where you want to be in a couple of months is important. So is where you hope to be in 5 or 10 years or even further in the future.
- ☐ Decide what characteristics of an employer are important to you. Evaluate potential employers against your criteria. Concentrate on those employers that best meet the criteria.

2

The recruiting
process on campus

The placement office

The success of any school's recruiting program depends on the quality of the services rendered by its placement office. Almost universally, colleges and graduate schools maintain a department whose sole purpose is to assist students in securing employment. Many placement offices also make their services available to graduates who find themselves in the job market.

The placement office advises students on the preparation of résumés and distributes the résumés to potential employers when requested to do so.

Another important service that the placement office should render is to hold training sessions in interviewing techniques open to any student who wishes to avail himself of the service. At such sessions videotapes of mock interviews are made so students can later observe their behavior during the interviews. Persons experienced in hiring should play the role of recruiter. If such persons are unavailable, it is not unusual

9

for corporations, on request, to send trained representatives to the school to help out for a day or two.

When a student sees and hears how he handles himself in a mock interview, he will learn much about himself and about how he comes across to the interviewer. In fact, this will be the first opportunity for many students to observe themselves in action as they try to sell themselves. The learning experience will be even greater if the interviewer watches a rerun of the tape with the student and makes comments as the interview progresses.

The placement office encourages a wide variety of organizations to schedule recruiting visits to the institution, with the result that hundreds of corporations recruit at major colleges and graduate schools.

Each organization is urged to provide information on itself. Annual reports, brochures, descriptions of job offerings, and other pertinent information are supplied. Companies that do not visit an institution because of cost considerations or limited recruiting requirements will supply company information and a list of specific job openings and will ask that students write, enclosing a résumé.

The placement office will prepare a file, available to students for study, on each company and will put appropriate notices on a bulletin board.

Ultimately, it will prepare a master schedule for recruiters and students will sign for interviews, which are usually 30 minutes in length.

A well-organized and efficient placement office can be of inestimable assistance to a student looking for the right job, and a college graduate who plans to attend graduate school will do well to inquire into the quality of the graduate school's placement office before he makes his final selection.

If an institution for some reason or other—usually lack of interest or unwillingness to provide the necessary funding—

does not have a well-organized and adequately staffed placement office, every student is being deprived of a service to which he or she should be entitled. It is my conviction that any educational institution, as a part of the training it provides for its students, should also be responsible for doing everything in its power to assist them in finding the right spot in which to enjoy the fruits of the course of study they have undertaken.

There are a few months of intensive activity for the placement department. The more efficient departments spend the rest of the year building relationships with potential employers, encouraging more and more companies to recruit at the school.

Smaller or more distant firms can be urged to acquaint the department of any jobs they might have to offer. To make such employers aware of the talent available, the placement office should collect in a book the résumés of graduating students and offer it to any company that wishes to purchase a copy. In addition to the résumés, the book will contain information on students' geographic preferences and fields of interest and will provide listings of undergraduate engineering and science majors. Thus, a medium-size company in Iowa that does not send a recruiter to a school can pinpoint an individual with a degree in electrical engineering who desires a job with a manufacturer in the Middle West.

Summer employment is always a problem for nongraduating students, and placement offices can do much in this area if they establish relationships with companies that habitually hire summer help for internships or special projects. They should also regard it as part of their service to educate companies to the value of offering summer jobs to nongraduating students. Far too few corporations are aware of the benefits to them of such a program.

Another important function of the placement office should

be the development of statistics relating to offers received and offers accepted by members of the graduating class. The salary levels and geographic origin of offers should be tabulated and constantly updated so that, during the recruiting season, students will know what price they should place on their services in various types of jobs in different areas of the country. Students should report when they have accepted an offer, but salary and the name of the lucky employer should be kept confidential.

At some time in the summer or fall a placement office should compile a full report on the performance in the job market of that spring's graduates. Not all of them entered the job market, and not all of those that did will report the results of their efforts. However, an excellent placement office will develop comprehensive figures that will be of great assistance to next year's graduates. Starting salaries will be broken down by industry, geographic location, type of work (sales, finance, research, production, and so forth), so that the following spring a student will know that in the previous year a New York bank paid an average salary of so much to fill a certain job, or $1,600 more than was paid by an Atlanta bank to fill a similar job. Comparing last year's results with early returns of the current year will enable graduates to determine the relative health of the job market and the effects of inflation on starting salaries.

The placement office should maintain a master index of all graduating students. When a student reports an offer, a notation should be made on his card and the details should be inputted (a horrible word) into the statistical record. When he reports the acceptance of an offer, his card should be removed from the open file. Thus, the placement office will have an up-to-date record of every graduate's status.

A student who goes through the recruiting process with little or no success should be offered assistance by the placement office. Perhaps his interviewing technique is poor, or perhaps he has personal characteristics that have penalized him—the placement office should advise all such students.

By graduation the number of students whose cards remain in the open file should have been reduced to a very few. Now is the time for the staff to earn its keep. The causes for a student's inability to secure a job should be analyzed and counseling sessions held, possible employers should be phoned or written, and everything else possible should be done to assist the unhired students.

Is the placement office at your institution functioning as it should? If so, you a lucky person and you made a wise choice of the school to attend. If not, is there anything that you and the other members of your class can do about it?

I'm all for placement offices, and I'm all for the institutions that staff them with qualified professionals who are strongly motivated to do the job they were hired to do.

The first interview—Meet the players

We will assume that your placement office has done its job properly and that over the next two months several hundred recruiters will descend on your ivied or redbrick towers. The curtain is about to go up on the opening scenes of the mating game.

Let's take a look at the players in this contest, for it is a contest, and don't you ever forget it.

On one side of the table sits the interviewer. Who is he, and what are his objectives?

We can start by saying that he has in his possession a job you might like to have. This fact makes him important to you. It is in your interest to speak and act respectfully toward him.

Perhaps he is a representative of his company's personnel department. I shouldn't have used that designation; nowadays such individuals are referred to as members of the human resources department. That is supposed to sound more dignified. To me it doesn't. Nevertheless, whatever we call him, he should be a trained interviewer. Notice that I said *should be*. Often he is not. You will meet many interviewers. A few will be real professionals; others will be adequate; but a few will do an injustice to you and the companies they represent.

What will a competent interviewer attempt to accomplish in a screening interview? He may have had the opportunity to study your résumé before he meets you for the first time. If not, he will glance over it for a few minutes to determine whether there is a fit between you and one of the jobs he is attempting to fill. His next objective, and probably the most important one, is to make a preliminary judgment as to how well you would fit into his organization. He will be concerned with your attitude, presence, personality, and appearance. He will be interested in how you handle yourself in a one-on-one situation, in how well you express yourself when answering questions or talking about yourself. He will attempt to discover whether you really want to work for his company or are merely practicing your interviewing technique. He will decide whether you are a highly motivated person with the ambition and potential to become a valuable asset to his company.

If his first impressions are favorable, he will attempt to demonstrate why it would be to your advantage to join his organization.

In short, the recruiter is both a buyer and a seller. He wants to pick the best of the applicants he sees, and at the same time he must extol the advantage to the applicant of choosing his company over others.

The role of the applicant is much simpler. He should not be interviewing if he is not attracted to the company and the opportunity it might afford him. Thus, he is no more or less than a salesman, and his purpose is to present himself to the recruiter in as favorable a light as possible. The résumé is his first selling point; it must be well prepared. Then, when the interview gets under way, he will attempt to display the merchandise he has to offer in the most convincing fashion possible.

His goal is not to receive a job offer on the spot. Wonders never cease, and there is no law that it can't happen, but the odds against such an event are astronomical. What the applicant does strive for is to pass the first cut. In a day an interviewer might talk to 15 men and women at a school and might visit 10 schools. Of the 150 applicants he meets, he may consider 20 to be worthy of serious consideration for one of the dozen or so jobs he has to offer in various departments of his company.

It is up to the applicant to make such a positive impression on the recruiter that he will be among those selected for a second series of interviews at the head office of the company.

Hints:

- First impressions are important. Always keep this in mind.
- Remember also that you have only half an hour in which to convince the recruiter that your application is worthy of further consideration.
- There is heavy competition for callback interviews. To be among the select few you must demonstrate the value of what you have to offer.

The interview—How to handle yourself

We're going to spend a lot of time on this subject, so prepare yourself for a long discussion. It should be unnecessary for me to tell you that how you conduct yourself during an interview is important to you. I'll mention it anyhow. The interview might be the beginning of a long and rewarding association with the recruiter's company; it will lead to nothing if you blow it. All you can do is be aware of the pitfalls that await you and handle yourself to the best of your ability.

So, let's get right to it.

We'll assume that the inquisition will take place in Room 242 of Founders Hall. You approach the closed door warily. Affixed to it is a sheet of paper stating that Mr. George Spencer is interviewing for XYZ Corporation. Below that statement is a schedule dividing the day into half-hour segments. Except for the hour reserved for lunch there isn't a blank space between 8:30 in the morning and 5 in the afternoon. Spencer has a busy day lined up. Your name appears in the 10 to 10:30 slot. You check your watch for the fifth time in the last 10 minutes and find you are 5 minutes early.

Hint:

□ Always be early for an interview, even though you know the interviewer is running late.

You hear the murmur of voices as you check the list. You take up a station a few feet from the door and again make sure you have an extra copy of your résumé should the interviewer have mislaid the one that the placement office gave him. You also assure yourself that a pencil and a piece of paper are available should you need them.

Hint:

□ Come fully prepared. Bring the necessary tools with you.

At three minutes after 10 the door opens and a classmate, looking flustered and with a sheen of perspiration on his brow, rushes past you, muttering to himself. You steel your nerves, step forward, and . . .

"Good morning. I'm George Spencer."

"Good morning, Mr. Spencer," you reply. "I'm Charles Reed." You are delighted that your voice, which has an unfortunate tendency to break in moments of stress, does not betray you on this occasion.

Mr. Spencer puts out his hand, and you clasp it in your own. Your grip should be firm, neither a dead fish nor a steel vise.

What happens if you put out your hand and he makes no move to take it? For the first time we are confronted with a basic fact of interviews. It is this: The interviewer is in the driver's seat. He, not you, is in control of what will happen in the next half hour. Many authorities on the subject state that since it is the applicant's interview, he should direct its course, control the situation. To me, this is unadulterated rubbish. It is the interviewer's room; he is the host. In addition, his company has positions to hand out and you want one. Furthermore, in most cases he is older and more experienced than you are. Finally, he is employed and you aren't. All of these facts lead me to conclude that the interviewer is the head man and that the applicant should fit his actions to the lead of the recruiter.

Thus, if the interviewer wants to shake hands, it is up to him to make the first move.

Hint:

□ Don't put out your hand until the interviewer extends his.

If the interviewer is a gentleman and reasonably mobile at that time of day, he will have risen to greet you or will have remained on his feet after parting with the previous applicant. He will probably sit down after greeting you, and he should ask you to be seated.

Hint:

□ Don't flop into a chair as soon as the interviewer sits. Wait to be invited.

What position do you adopt when you do sit? Good question. Behaviorists have a field day when they talk about body language. Do you place an ankle on the other knee and lean back in an arrogant devil-may-care posture? Do you lean forward, a flinty glint in your eye, with elbows placed aggressively on the table between you and the interviewer? I'm no expert on body language, and I have no interest in becoming one. I do, however, have strong feelings on the matter.

Hints:

□ Sit in a relaxed manner, neither lolling back in the chair nor poised on its front edge as if about to launch yourself into space.

□ Cross your feet, if you will, but don't cross your legs.

□ Keep your hands quietly in your lap, not plunged into jacket pockets.

□ Don't allow your hands to fuss with neckties, hair, or earrings.

Again, let the interviewer be your guide. Follow his example so long as it is worthy of emulation. If the interview proceeds smoothly and good rapport is established, he may relax after a few minutes. So, then, may you, but never relax too much. An interview is a formal occasion, and you should always be on your best behavior.

Another point comes to mind. When the interviewer asks you to sit down, he may use your first name. Suppose he says, "Sit down, Mary," and adds, "May I call you Mary?" Your answer should be, "Thank you. Please do." Notice, Mary does not say, "Thank you, George."

While it is proper for the interviewer to use your first name as a friendly gesture employed to put you at your ease, it is not proper for you to assume that he wishes you to use his first name unless he specifically asks you to do so. Follow this advice even though he is only a couple of years older than you or your own age. He could even be younger than you, but that has no bearing on the matter. He may be a vice president of his company, and the only people there who use his given name may be a few equals and the chief executive officer. The interviewer may be an earlier graduate of your school and a member of your fraternity or sorority. Even then, you maintain a formal relationship with him until he directs you otherwise. The only exception to this rule is made when you have known the interviewer in the past. In such a circumstance you use the form of address you habitually employ.

Hint:

☐ Irrespective of whether the interviewer calls you by your first or your last name, always refer to him or her as Mr. Spencer, Mrs. Spencer, or Miss Spencer, whichever the case may be.

Mr. Spencer has done enough interviewing to know that you are understandably somewhat nervous. Therefore, he spends a moment or two putting you at ease. He does this by making a comment about the weather, the beauty of the campus, or a headline in the morning paper. The applicant replies politely but does not turn his answer into a compulsive monologue. Don't be abrupt, but always remember the serious purpose of the interview.

The amenities having been observed, the interview commences.

"Tell me about yourself, Mary," he says.

Now, you're on your own. The ball is in your court. He

has your résumé in front of him, and he may be looking at it as you talk. On the other hand, he may be looking directly at you.

It would be a horrible mistake to start your reply like this. "I was born on July 6 in South Bend, Indiana, 21 years ago and went to grade school on North Avenue. After that I attended junior high at . . ."

Take a minute to think. Why did he ask the question? Perhaps to get you talking about something with which you ought to be thoroughly familiar. His purpose may be to ease your tension. In addition, he wants to find out what kind of a person you are—information not included in your résumé—and most of all he wants to discover how well you express yourself. Do you talk easily, interestingly? How cultured is your grammar, diction? Do you use slang? Do you look at the interviewer as you talk to him? Are your hands as active as your mouth? Do you seem to be thinking as you talk, listening to yourself?

Hint:

□ Never forget that the impression you make is probably more important to the interviewer than your grade average.

A slight digression. I have just read an article in a college alumni magazine in which an unsuccessful candidate for a Rhodes scholarship tells of his trials and tribulations during a regional meeting with the scholarship committee. He recounts his efforts to rid his speech of such expressions as "you know," "for sure," "yeah," "like," and "bummer." It hadn't been easy. In this respect he made it through the interview with flying colors, and later, after learning of his rejection, he commiserated with another unsuccessful candidate who remarked that his most cherished dream had just been shattered. Our hero replied, "Yeah, what a bummer. You know?" Do as he did, and avoid such expressions until the interview is concluded. I hope you'll be more successful than he was, but if he got that far in the competition, he'll do all right, you know.

Now, back to our interview. Mary is a college senior with little prior work experience. What does she say if she doesn't supply a year-by-year chronicle of her life or repeat what is contained in her résumé?

Hint:

□ She supplies information that will do more than merely inform. It will also give insights into favorable facets of her character and personality.

How about if she starts this way?

We are a large family—I have five brothers and sisters—and we are all very close. My father works for the government, and by the time I came to college we had moved four times. I keep in touch with friends all over the country. When I was 16, we went to Rome for two years. I became fascinated with Roman history—history is my college major—and I became fluent in Italian.

What has Mary done in a few words? She has put several messages across. She comes from what is probably a well-adjusted family. She is accustomed to change; she makes friends wherever she lives, has intellectual curiosity, and speaks Italian like a native. If Mary is smart, and by now I am sure she is, she will talk with animation. She will enjoy discussing her family and her life. Mr. Spencer is already two thirds sold on her.

Hint:

□ Your answer should have a dual purpose—to inform and to reveal the real you.

Let us now consider how a candidate for a master's degree in business administration in a well-known southern institution might answer the same question. He worked for three years in a bank before going back to school. Suppose he began this way.

I grew up in a small town in Iowa and went to college a hundred miles from home. When I graduated, I looked for a job in Chicago as I wanted to find out what life was like in a big city. I did well at the bank—they gave me a title in my third year—but I began to realize how little I knew about the theory and practice of management. It was clear that a degree in business administration was essential if I was to achieve my career objective. I chose this school because I wanted to be exposed to a different part of the country—many of the students here are Southerners, and I had met very few in Iowa or Chicago. My present desire is to get into the field of financial planning, and I feel that my experience and education equip me to enter the area. Later on I want to move into general management on an executive level.

Like Mary, our candidate is enthusiastic, speaks with conviction, and talks directly to the interviewer, not to the floor or to the wall behind the interviewer.

What has our friend accomplished? He has made the following points:

1. He came from a rural environment.
2. He had the initiative to broaden his experience by going to Chicago.
3. He was successful there.
4. He was ambitious enough to realize he was handicapped by his lack of knowledge.
5. He did something about it, and at the same time he exposed himself to a new environment.
6. He had developed short- and long-term career goals and had decided on a path to reach them.

Again, we must admire our applicant. He has answered the question, but he has done so in terms that give the interviewer an insight into what makes him tick.

Hints:

□ Answer the question posed to you, but answer it in a way that gives you an opportunity to tell what kind of person you are.

□ Remember that you are a salesman. All you have to sell is yourself. Pick out your best qualities—incorporate a description of them in your answer.

□ Weave the points you want to make into a natural story about yourself.

□ Above all—be prepared. Nearly all interviewers will make some form of request that you tell them about yourself. Work on your reply. Practice it, and don't be afraid to make changes if parts of the reply don't go over too well with an interviewer. The next interviewer might like the revised version.

□ Again—preparation and practice.

Aggressive and assertive

Let's spend a little time with these two words. They bother me. Male applicants may state that they are aggressive; young women pride themselves on their assertiveness. What do the words mean?

Aggression describes a forceful action, such as an unprovoked attack, usually for the purpose of dominating. It connotes injurious behavior. An aggressive person is often quarrelsome. The Soviet invasion of Afghanistan was an act of aggression. Does the applicant wish to give the interviewer the impression that he is Attila the Hun?

The word does have another meaning: enterprising, marked by forceful energy and initiative. These are excellent qualities that will impress the interviewer. But, do we know what the word means to him? If you state that you are an aggressive person, will he regard you as a descendant of the Assyrians who swept down like the wolf on the fold or as an energetic young person loaded with initiative. Who knows?

Assertive is defined as a synonym of aggressive. It connotes a positive and forceful statement, usually in anticipation of denial or objection. Asserting one's rights usually contains an element of belligerency. "Nobody is going to push me around, and you better believe it!" Is that the impression you want to give of yourself? I think not.

No one wants to be a patsy, a Caspar Milquetoast everyone imposes on. But, you don't have to walk around with a chip on your shoulder, and to many people assertiveness conveys just such an impression.

Aggressive and assertive people are hard to get along with. They rock boats. Who wants an individual around who tramples underfoot any person standing in his way or reacts violently to every imagined affront? Who would hire such an individual? Would you? Thus, I suggest that you expunge the words *aggressive* and *assertive* from your vocabulary while interviewing.

Yet, you are enterprising and energetic and you have a full complement of initiative. Furthermore, you are not a 90-pound weakling who gets sand kicked in his face at the beach. How do you get your message across to your listener without turning him off?

Hints:

□ Realize that listeners will not always define words as you do.

Be clear when you express your thoughts. Ensure against mis-interpretation.

☐ If you are aggressive and assertive in the worst sense of the words, say so, and be prepared for a quick and unsatisfactory termination of the interview. (Your first assignment should be to break yourself of these unfortunate characteristics.)

☐ If you are enterprising and energetic, use those words to describe yourself.

☐ If you have a mind of your own and won't be stampeded or trampled underfoot, say so in pleasant terms, and smile when you say it.

3

Questions and answers

A recruiter often finds it difficult to get an applicant to talk freely and in a relaxed manner. He is sensitive to the applicant's ease or unease as he speaks. Does the applicant appear relaxed and comfortable as he talks? Does he look at the interviewer? Is there a smile on his face or a look of abject terror exacerbated by telltale beads of perspiration on a furrowed brow?

Thus, the interviewer's earlier questions, such as "Tell me about yourself," are designed to put the applicant at ease and to start him talking.

Multilevels in questions and answers

Many experts claim that the art of management consists of determining what questions to ask. That statement might not be totally accurate, but it is undeniable that once the real interview starts, the skilled interviewer asks questions that will reveal characteristics of the applicant. The questions will be double- or triple-barreled; the interviewer seeks answers to specific questions and is also alert to insights into the personality of the individual he is interviewing as revealed by the answers. Furthermore, he may attach as much weight to what the applicant does not say as he does to what is said.

In similar fashion, the answers given by the applicant are also multileveled. If he is alert, the answers will cover the overt questions, but the applicant will phrase them in a manner that will point up strengths in his personality and at the same time will avoid exposing possible weaknesses. Confusing, isn't it? Who's outsmarting whom?

Let's see how it works.

Solitary versus group work

Question: Do you prefer to work on your own or in a group?

Is this a simple, innocuous question? Don't you believe it. The interviewer wants to know:

1. Which method of working do you prefer?
2. Are you a loner who is not comfortable in a group?
3. Are you a take-charge person who resents the element of control and discipline inherent in a group effort?
4. Are you dependent on others to take charge and direct you?
5. Are you an overly aggressive individual whose personality is so abrasive that you can't get along with others?

Even though the interviewer has asked for the answer to the first question, the other four are the important ones to him. Insidious, isn't it? Yet, all the answers are needed if the interviewer is to have a good reading on your personality.

How should you answer? The worst answer you could make would be a simple statement such as "I prefer to work alone." Such a reply cannot be faulted as a plain statement of fact, but it has nothing else to recommend it. It ignores the covert questions and gives the interviewer no feeling for your personality or character. Suppose you phrased your answer like this.

> Basically, I prefer to work on my own. I set very high standards for myself, enjoy responsibility, and have faith in my analytical skills and judgment. On the other hand, I realize that many decisions cannot be made by an individual and that it is often essential to work with others. I have always gotten along well with people, and although I prefer being in charge of a group, I have found that I can accept direction and work harmoniously when someone else is the leader.

You've hit the jackpot. The interviewer has the answers to his direct question as well as the implied questions he will not have to voice aloud. And, your answer not only indicates that you perceive the underlying concerns of the interviewer but also gives a favorable impression of your personality.

Analyze your response. How many of your strengths are revealed in your 30-second answer? You have listed at least six favorable aspects of your character, and, equally important, you have shown an ability to smoke out what is involved in a tricky question. Your answer has been to the point, but you have also used it as a vehicle to put the assets you have to offer a potential employer in a favorable light.

Hints:

□ Never answer a question in a word or two.

□ Be perceptive of what the interviewer really wants to know.

□ Answer the unasked questions.

□ Make sure your answers point up your strengths and don't expose your possible weaknesses.

□ No matter what you say—be honest. Example: If you can't

tolerate working with others, don't say you enjoy it. Find
something else to talk about.

Why our company?

Question: Why do you want to work for XYZ Corporation?

Do you answer, "Um, uh, it's a well-known big company,
you know." I hope not. What does the interviewer really
want to find out? Simple. Have you done your homework?
Let's go back a bit. Since XYZ is one of the Fortune 500,
copies of its most recent annual report have been sent to
your placement office. So also have pamphlets explaining
XYZ's employment policies and outlines of XYZ job openings that will be available.

An interviewer will probably ask this question to discover
whether you have studied the material on file. If you haven't,
he will conclude that you are not really serious about wanting to work for the company. He will also be alert to evidence
that your research has gone beyond the data supplied. Perhaps yesterday's *Wall Street Journal* carried an article on the
company or industry that you might refer to in your answer.
The interviewer will also want to discover whether you have
actually related your education or your prior experience to
the qualifications required to fill one of the jobs he has to
offer.

Your answer perhaps will start with this last point, and you
will mention your college major field and relate it to the position in which you are interested. You will display knowledge
of the company's various divisions, of the areas in which expansion is projected and how this affects your choice of the
openings available. You will match your skills and strengths
to a particular position and demonstrate how the position

provides an excellent match between the company and yourself. The more you know about the company and the job, the stronger will be your sales pitch.

Hints:

- Study all material supplied by the company, and demonstrate your familiarity with it.
- Ferret out additional information on the company.
- Study the descriptions of the jobs that the company is offering.
- Match yourself with a specific position.
- Get your act together in a smooth, natural presentation.
- Don't come over too strong in spouting your knowledge. The interviewer knows far more about his company than you do.
- Prepare and rehearse your answer beforehand. It's a sure thing that you will find a use for it.

Work experience

Question: Tell me about your previous work experience.

Let's assume you are an about-to-be-graduated college senior. The interviewer has your résumé before him, and it lists the summer jobs you have held. On the surface they aren't very impressive. After graduating from high school, you were a counselor at a summer camp. Following your freshman year you were a lifeguard at a municipal swimming pool for children, and the last two summers you caddied at the country club in your hometown. You might think that these credentials do not prepare you for a selling job with IBM. However, when we look below the surface, we find a number of positive statements you can make that will impress the interviewer. It is all a matter of how you phrase your answer.

Hints:

- Never start with an apology. Don't say, "Well, I've never had a real job, but . . ."
- Be positive and stress the value of what you have done.

So, you might frame your answer like this:

When I was in grammar school, I had a paper route, and I kept it all through high school. The job covered my spending money, and I saved enough to handle some of my expenses in my first year at college. At the camp and at the swimming pool I learned how to get along with younger children and earn their respect. Both jobs taught me a lot about assuming responsibility.

The last two summers I caddied. That was hard work—it gets hot at home in the summer—but I earned more money as a caddy than I could get on any other job, and that was important to me. In addition, I got to know a lot of the professional men at the club and a number of them asked specifically for me. Incidentally, I learned to enjoy golf and the club pro let me practice early in the morning and in the evening when the course was empty. Caddies were allowed to play Monday mornings, and I improved to the point where I had several rounds in the 70s last summer.

I worked two nights a week and every other weekend while I was in college and was able to pay almost half of my expenses.

Contrast that answer with this.

Well, as a kid I had a paper route, and in the last four summers I worked in a summer camp, was a lifeguard, and caddied. The money came in handy while I was in college.

The facts are the same, but what a difference there is in their presentation.

What will be the interviewer's probable reaction to the preferred answer? He will have learned that you:

1. Probably do not come from a wealthy family.
2. Learned the value and use of money at an early age.

3. Learned how to get along with people.
4. Learned how to earn respect and assume responsibility.
5. Worked hard to develop your talents. The interviewer has probably been playing golf for 20 years and never come close to breaking 80.
6. Are a conscientious and motivated person.

If I were the IBM recruiter I would hire you. Good luck on your job.

Are you getting the drift? Are you beginning to see how questions are to be answered? You should be.

Hints:

□ Answers should disclose favorable aspects of your character.
□ A well-prepared and carefully constructed answer will impress the interviewer. He will know what you are doing—he's no dummy—and he appreciates a fellow professional when he meets one.

What other questions might an interviewer ask? You will find that perhaps a dozen will crop up again and again during interviews. If you're smart, you'll have your answers prepared ahead of time. Let's analyze more of the questions you are likely to encounter.

Strengths

Question: What do you consider to be your major strengths?

That is a very simple query, but we ask ourselves what kind of answer the interviewer is looking for; what strengths will appeal to him.

Suppose you answer,

I'm very smart. I made Phi Beta Kappa in my junior year, and my old man is president of the biggest bank in the state.

Very impressive, no doubt, but hardly what the interviewer wants to hear. Why not? What's wrong with having the smarts and a father who is a big wheel? Nothing, really, but what impression might such a statement convey? The interviewer could feel you were arrogant about your brains and also trying to impress him with the importance of your parent. He might feel you were evidencing a superior attitude that would make you undesirable as an employee of his company.

Let us suppose that you are a young woman graduating from college this spring and that you have had no previous work experience. You might frame your answer this way.

We are a large family. I have three older brothers and a younger sister. At an early age we were made responsible for certain chores around the house, and we were expected to take care of them without having to be reminded every day. In school and college I have always been conscientious, and I take pride in doing the best possible job on every assignment. I am a class officer and an editor of the college paper. I have a number of friends, and I get along well with people. I would say I set very high standards for myself, and up to now, at least, I have been satisfied with my performance in everything I have undertaken.

Low key? I think so, but every word has a ring of confidence, motivation, and good solid worth. Here is a young woman without any work experience to speak of, yet she certainly possesses many of the qualities necessary for becoming a valuable and promotable employee.

Hints:

- Coming on too strong turns people off.
- Don't recite a laundry list of the 20 most desirable characteristics.

□ Focus on a few essentials, and give examples.

□ Show yourself in a favorable light, but don't present yourself as a combination of Einstein, Joan of Arc, and George Washington.

□ Be honest, but look at the brighter side of yourself.

Weaknesses

Question: You have told me about your strengths, but few of us are perfect. Would you let me know what you consider to be your weaknesses?

The interviewer has a benign smile on his face when he poses this question. He is really interested in your answer, and his interest is not only in your weaknesses as you disclose them but also in the manner in which you handle the question.

Should you answer by saying, "I am not aware that I have any serious weaknesses"? I would not recommend it. Should you look your inquisitor squarely in the eye and state baldly, "I habitually get smashed every Saturday night; I kick stray dogs and make passes at every attractive bird I see." I wouldn't advise it. There must be a better answer.

In high school I was close to the top of my class and played on three teams. Things seemed to come very easy to me, and I suppose I became a little intolerant of others. In college I found that many of my classmates were smarter than I and better athletes as well. This taught me to be a little more understanding of people. I have much more respect for others now.

That's a good answer. It admits a weakness, but what is much more important, it shows that the individual became aware of the weakness and did something to correct it. By doing so, he made himself a better person.

I worked in a bank for two years after graduating from college and discovered that my weakness in accounting and financial areas would make it difficult for me to advance as rapidly or as far as I wanted. As a result I enrolled in graduate school, and I now feel fully competent to handle any assignment that might be given me.

Great. The individual recognized a weakness, did something about it, and has turned the weakness into a strength.

A young woman says,

I have always been overly conscientious. I was never satisfied with my class preparation or my written assignments unless I did a nearly perfect job. As a result I had trouble meeting deadlines, and this became a serious problem. I finally realized I had not been making the best use of my time and also that nothing will ever be perfect. As a result I discovered I could get my work done on schedule, maintain high standards, and at the same time take pride in my work.

That young lady has learned an important lesson—she is maturing. At some time design must be frozen and production started.

Here's another answer.

As an engineering major, I have to do a tremendous amount of technical reading. I was a relatively slow reader, and this proved to be a serious handicap, so last year I enrolled in a speed-reading course and I have been working on it ever since. I am still not the world's fastest reader, but now I can read in an hour what used to take me an hour and a half.

Again, he saw a weakness and he did something about it.

Hints:

□ Never blab about unfortunate personal characteristics.

□ Never mention a weakness unless you also make clear that you recognized it and did something to correct it.

□ Don't refuse to acknowledge the fact that you are human.

"I may have some weaknesses, but I prefer to focus on my strengths rather than my shortcomings." That attitude won't do at all.

□ Remember that an important element in your answer is the manner in which you field the question.

Other companies

Question: What other companies are you interviewing with?

Does the interviewer really care what specific companies you are applying to? Possibly. What does he really want to know? Simple. Have you a job or career objective, or are you merely playing the field? What is the rationale of your job hunt program? Makes sense, doesn't it?

Suppose you answer like this.

I am seeking an opportunity in the field of international banking, and I prefer a job in New York, which is the financial headquarters of the world. I plan to interview with Citibank, Chase, Chemical, Manufacturers Hanover, and Bankers Trust.

What have you told the interviewer? You have a clear career plan, you know where you want to work, and you know the major organizations in the field. If you impress the interviewer at your meeting with him, he will know that if he wants you, he is up against top competition for your services.

Suppose you answer this way.

I am looking for an opportunity in brand management with a large top-quality organization. Since I am single, where I live isn't as important to me as the opportunity. I intend to interview with General Foods, Procter & Gamble, General Mills, and Colgate.

Good answer. You know what you want, and you don't care whether you live in White Plains, Cincinnati, Minneapolis, or New York.

There is a basic difference between these answers and a haphazard list of unrelated companies.

Hints:

☐ Give an answer compatible with your career choice.

☐ Know what you are looking for and why.

☐ Be consistent.

Pressure

Question: Do you work well under pressure?

Hell, yes! The tougher the going, the better I like it. Last November we were down 26-0 against State with six minutes left on the clock. I threw four touchdown passes, and we pulled it out 28 to 26.

I know there are people like that—I read about them in the Sunday paper. If you are one of them, I suggest you get a job with that chap who travels the world putting out oil well fires. Even better, get yourself elected president of the United States, and more power to you. Most of us aren't that self-assured, and it's probably a good thing—for the rest of us, that is.

On the other hand, the interviewer certainly doesn't expect you to blurt out, "I freeze up, am incoherent, and get sick to my stomach."

He does want to find out whether you can be expected to keep your cool when exposed to stress, whether you continue to function or freeze when the heat is on. (Why should anyone freeze when occupying the hot seat?) He would also like to know whether you have considered the subject and have a ready answer.

A college senior might reply in this fashion.

That's not an easy question to answer. I have participated in sports all my life and developed a strong competitive spirit. I always felt I played my best in critical situations. Sports pressure is different from pressure on the job, but I've met course deadlines, and I've been satisfied with my performance when several requirements have hit me at the same time.

That individual, man or woman, has had little experience outside sports and the classroom, but the interviewer will appreciate that fact and, I should think, approve the answer. I would not suggest that an applicant rely wholly on competitive sports for his answer. In college, did you have to earn a portion of your expenses? Did you hold time-consuming offices involving substantial responsibility during your college career? As a result, were you forced to allocate your time and discipline your behavior? If so, tell the interviewer about it. In doing so, you will not only answer his question, but you will also demonstrate that you are a mature, dependable person.

An MBA candidate has a ready-made answer.

At this school a student is expected to devote 60 to 80 hours a week to the course. This goes on week after week. During my college days and the three years I worked before coming back to school, there were occasional periods of high pressure but nothing like my experience here. Very soon I discovered that to cope I had to learn to discipline myself, to get the greatest possible value out of my time. I made the adjustment satisfactorily and now feel able to handle any pressure situation I may be involved in.

Hints:

□ A three- or four-word answer won't do.

□ Use any ammunition you can find in your past to support your point.

□ Frame your answer so it refers to other desirable traits that you possess.

□ There is pressure in every interview. Show you can handle it.

Friends

Question: Do you make friends easily?

Be careful of this one. Don't make yourself out to be a good-time Charlie, the little friend of all the world. There is a difference between friends and acquaintances. Be aware of the distinction. Will Rogers said he had never met a man he didn't like. I and many others are not as compassionate.

I would say I have three or four good friends. A friendship takes time to develop. It requires a blend of common interest and personality. On the other hand, I get along with people well and I have dozens of acquaintances—people whom I enjoy being with and who seem to enjoy my company.

What have you done? You have made a point, explained it, and then gone beyond the specific question and offered additional relevant information.

Hints:

□ Give a thinking person's answer, not the first reply that comes to mind.

□ Show that you have taste and discrimination.

Questions that have no answers

Question: If you were the president of Chrysler, what would you do?

The interviewer who asks a question like that one ought to be drawn and quartered. Does he expect you to think for a few seconds and then offer a well-organized and explicit plan for the complete restoration of a sick giant? Does he expect you to present better strategies than those offered by the chief executive officer of the moment? Not at all. All he wants to find out is how you react to a difficult question on a subject on which you cannot be expected to be an expert. Incidentally, he may recall your answer to his query on working under pressure and compare your reply with your reaction to that question.

"I'd let the company buy up my contract, take my money to Florida, and go fishing." That answer has much to recommend it, but it will hardly endear you to the interviewer.

How about this?

Chrysler is faced with serious financial problems, and I have neither the experience nor the knowledge required of that company's president. If I had to take the position, I would attempt to cut costs and at the same time improve quality and service. Also, I'd hire the best financial and automotive brains I could find.

How does the answer come across? You take a realistic view of your inability to handle such a job, yet you do have a couple of sensible suggestions.

Hints:

□ Realize what the interviewer is really asking.

□ Don't try to be all things to all people.

□ Have a realistic understanding of your abilities and your inabilities.

Long-range plans

Question: Where would you like to be in 20 years?

What is the purpose of this question? Probably to discover whether you have a career plan or whether you are a drifter with no specific objective in mind. The question will elicit different answers from a college graduate than it would from a candidate for a master's degree in business administration.

Can a young man or woman, graduating in a few months from college, with little business experience, be expected to know where he or she will be in 20 years? I should think not. Thus, were I in that position, I might answer,

I am interested in a position with a company in the energy field, and I would like to start in the marketing division. As I gain experience and acquire a better understanding of my talents, I might switch into the financial planning area, where my marketing experience would be of value. Because of my inexperience I can't plot a specific course so far ahead, but I do have ambition and a desire to succeed. As my ability develops, I expect to gravitate toward the area where my strengths will be most useful to the company and me.

I like that answer. I am inexperienced, but I know where I want to start; I am highly motivated, and the future will show me where my career path should lead me. Note the smart touch at the end of the answer. The applicant is not thinking only about himself—he is also thinking about the company.

The master's candidate with several years of work experience after college should have a much better understanding of his expectations and a much clearer career path in view. Such an individual might answer this way.

My previous experience in the marketing division of General Foods made me realize that I want to return to brand management after I graduate. I have emphasized marketing and financial management in my choice of electives. Ultimately, I would like to assume a position of authority in the area of finance, where my basic experience in marketing will be an important asset to the company and me.

The farther along the career path you are, the more specific will be your objectives. An answer that exudes confidence in one's abilities is desirable, but don't overdo it. "I expect to be a vice president in 15 years and president before I am 50." Certainly confident, but brash.

Hints:

□ Adapt your answer to the state of your situation and experience.

□ Show confidence in your ability, but don't come across as an arrogant know-it-all.

□ Don't ignore benefits to your employer as you proceed along your chosen career path.

Question: After working two years at the bank, why did you resign and enter business school?

This question will not be put to you if you are a college senior, but it won't hurt you to read what follows, since it might apply to you four years from now.

This is one of the few instances in which the interviewer really wants to know the answer to the specific question and has no ulterior motive in asking it. To reply, "I wasn't getting anywhere, so I thought I'd better go back to school to get more education," won't impress the interviewer with your desirability as an employee. An equally inferior answer is, "I realized that most of the top officers had an MBA, so I thought I might as well get one too."

I always intended to go to a business school, but I was advised to work a couple of years to gain practical business experience and maturity before starting the course. My work experience reinforced my decision to get an MBA. I went through the regular bank training program for six months. It included time as a teller and in the record keeping department before I was assigned to the consumer credit division. It didn't take me long to realize I knew almost nothing about the principles of accounting, marketing, financial management, and quantitative analysis. I feel I did well at my job—when I told my boss I was resigning, he said that if I stayed I would soon be given a title. As a matter of fact, the bank has already made me an offer to return. I plan to reject it.

My bank experience was invaluable to me. It taught me what business was all about, and it gave me a strong base for my studies here. Now, I have refined my career objectives and feel fully qualified to handle the job opportunity we have been discussing. I am confident of my ability to move ahead in your company and increase my value to you. My outlook is much broader; I know what it takes to succeed in business, and I now have the necessary equipment.

A blockbuster of an answer. Is it too long, too heavy? At a normal rate of speaking it would take about a minute and a half to deliver—5 percent of the interview time—but let us see what the answer accomplished.

1. It established the fact that you had a basic career plan when you finished college—work experience followed by graduate school.
2. It indicated that you had done well on the job—expectation of a title soon and an offer to return to the bank.
3. It showed how your development in graduate school resulted in a redefinition of your career aims.
4. It evidenced your maturity and confidence in your ability to succeed.

Each of the qualities you displayed is a strong point in your favor. These are the qualities an interviewer is looking for in an applicant.

Hints:

□ When fielding a question of this nature, don't give a day-to-day account of your life to date.

□ Do indicate a basic awareness of the underlying purpose of the question.

□ An answer is too long only if it lacks relevance.

□ Don't forgo an opportunity to blow your horn, but blow it unobtrusively, not stridently.

Psychological tests

Question: Will you take a series of psychological tests that we offer to applicants?

You won't be asked the question unless the tests are required of all applicants. Your answer can be either yes or no. If you do not approve of psychological testing, more and more companies are beginning to agree with you. But, even if you don't approve, the job opportunity may be so attractive that you will make the necessary concession. If your convictions about testing are so strong that you cannot violate them, say no to the interviewer, thank him for his courtesy, and don't waste any more of his or your time.

Hint:

□ Don't attempt to debate the issue with the interviewer. If his company has an inflexible rule about testing, he is unable to waive it.

The interviewer's company

Question: Is there anything you would like to know about my company?

Should the interviewer be a representative of General Motors, he would be understandably nonplussed if the applicant answers, "What do you make other than Cadillacs and Chevrolets?" Equally distressing to him would be, "No, I know all about General Motors."

What is the interviewer looking for in a reply? Well, first off, he wants to know whether you have done your homework. Are you familiar with the material he forwarded to the placement office a month ago? Have you kept up with recent industry or company news in the papers? If you were interviewing with IBM or American Telephone, a question regarding the company's attitude toward suits and government hearings would not be out of order. These suits and hearings have been well publicized, and their outcome will have a serious effect on the future of the company. If you were interviewing with a company that was not a giant and full information was unavailable to you, it would be proper for you to ask questions about the background of executives, family involvement in management, competitive position in specific areas, and attitude toward research and development.

It is also proper to ask any interviewer about company policies on new employees. "How long does the training period last?" "Are exceptions made, dependent on previous experience?" "When could I expect a permanent assignment?"

You might even probe close to sensitive areas. "What percentage of new employees like myself leave the company within a year or two?" "Can you give me any idea why they leave?" Job-hopping is a fact of life—applicants and interviewers are aware of the problem, and no individual can be faulted for wanting to know what the company experience has been in this respect.

Hints:

□ Let your questions show you have done your homework.
□ Ask questions that would have a bearing on your future should you take a job with the company.
□ Don't show off and try to embarrass the interviewer. "Tell me, how come the vice president in the XYZ Division just

got convicted in a price-fixing scandal." Such a question won't endear you to the interviewer, who was as distressed as the rest of management by the mis-behavior of a single individual in a small division of a well-respected corporation.

☐ Make sure that your questions show you are a serious and interested candidate for a job with the company.

☐ In a first interview, never, never ask about holidays, vacations, work hours, or salary. There is no place for such questions in a screening interview.

The subject of salary will be discussed at great length in Chapter 7. But, what can you say if the interviewer broaches the issue? Let us consider that right now.

Salary

Question: What salary do you think you are worth?

Don't ever come back with an exact figure or even a broad range. This is an unfair and improper question. The interviewer is either inexperienced or inept. He may even be trying to put you on the spot. Don't play his game if he is. The job you are discussing is worth a specific amount to the company, and when and if an offer is made, that will be the amount offered. Perhaps the amount will be adjusted because of the specific qualifications or experience of the candidate. In addition, the base salary is only a part of the whole package offered by the company. Benefits and the retirement program are quantitative factors that must also be considered, while promotion policy and cost of living at the job location are only two of the qualitative factors that should be considered in evaluating the position.

Given the need to consider such factors, how can a candidate be expected to put a value on his services? If he is foolish enough to mention a figure below what the company would otherwise offer, he has certainly done himself a disservice. If he has an inflated impression of his value and quotes a figure thousands of dollars higher than the amount the company expects to pay, he will seriously weaken his candidacy for the position.

What answer can a candidate give? The answer must be polite and sensible, yet it must not put the candidate in an untenable position. Here, again, an inexperienced college senior would not give the same answer as would be given by an organic chemist with a master's degree in business preceded by three years' experience with a drug company.

Let us suppose you are a young woman graduating with a bachelor's degree. You majored in art history, and you minored in economics. You spent three summers in New York, two of them in an art museum and one as an assistant analyst in a brokerage house. The position you are applying for is in the planning office of an oil company in Tulsa. Could you answer the question this way?

It is difficult for me to know what my salary should be. I know nothing about the cost of living in Tulsa. I have little knowledge of the employment policies of your company, and as yet I don't have much definite information on the opportunities offered by the job we are discussing. Salary is important to me—I'll need at least enough to live on—but I want to enjoy a happy and productive career. The responsibilities of the job and the possibility of advancement are equally important to me. I'd much rather postpone a definite answer until a later discussion.

Not bad. Our young friend has handled the situation admirably. She has offered several reasons why she cannot give a specific answer to the question, and at the same time she has given a clear impression that she is a highly motivated and serious woman interested in a successful career. She has made a wise suggestion—that the matter be dropped until a second interview that might be arranged at a later date in Tulsa. The suggestion conveys the impression that she is deeply interested in the position.

How would the interviewer respond to this answer? If he wished to pursue the matter, he would first have to supply the missing information. That might take him half an hour— time he doesn't have. He could not fail to be impressed by the smooth, reasonable method by which the applicant finessed a sticky question. Top score for our friend.

How about our organic chemist with his MBA and three years' experience with Eli Lilly. He is interviewing for a position as analyst with a top Wall Street investment banking firm. His qualifications would enable him to become very quickly a senior analyst of the drug industry. He might respond:

We are discussing a field which I feel highly qualified to enter. I checked with our placement office and found that last year the average salary for openings of this nature was $_____. Inflation will affect this year's offers. In addition, my familiarity with the drug industry should place a premium on my value. Again, New York has a high cost-of-living index. I am interviewing with several investment bankers and would expect all offers to be competitive.

We could say that this gentleman is aware of his value, and we would be quite right if we did. He is one man who will not sell himself short. Does he come across too strong? Is he, perhaps, a trifle arrogant? It is a tough field he is entering, and the faint of heart need not apply—they'll never know what hit them.

We will agree that he has done his homework. He has checked the placement office, and he has an accurate gauge of last year's offers. In his mind he has adjusted the figure for inflation and added a few thousand for his unique experience and background. The interviewer will realize that his company is not the only pebble on the beach. The law of supply and demand puts the applicant in an advantageous position, and he is aware of it. How different he is from the first applicant we discussed. Yet, you will observe that neither applicant made any attempt to put an explicit value on the services offered.

Hints:

- In a first interview, never mention the salary you want.
- Don't merely say, "I don't know what I am worth."
- Give reasons for your inability to answer the question directly.
- At the same time, take every opportunity that is offered to talk about your qualifications, whatever they are, and your motivations.

More about salary

The whole matter of salary is a tough one to handle. Suppose the interviewer puts his query this way.

Question: What would be your reaction if we offered you $_____?

Even now, you should not give a direct answer, though the offer may be far above your fondest dream. You will be equally mum if the offer is much lower than the amount you would be willing to accept.

Our relatively inexperienced art history major might say:

I have no real basis for a reaction. I don't know what the average offer will be this year for people in my position. I have been informed by the placement office of the average salary last year in your industry, but it is too early for me to know what other companies are offering.

She would then mention the other factors that would affect her thinking on this matter (see her answer to the previous question). She might conclude by saying that later on in the hiring season, after she has had an opportunity to talk with other prospective employers, she would be in a better position to give a more specific answer.

The experienced MBA chemist would probably respond in line with his answer to the original question.

Competent interviewers will not ask questions about salary in a screening interview. All interviewers are not experienced, however: some may be as inexperienced as the applicants they interview.

Hints:

- □ Don't allow yourself to be backed into a specific answer on salary.
- □ Finesse with grace all the interviewer's questions on the subject.
- □ Indicate that you would be better able to discuss the subject at future meetings.

Why you?

Question: Why should we hire you?

An applicant should draw a sigh of relief when he hears this question. It is an invitation to show the fit between the job and himself, to enlarge upon his talents, and above all to show his enthusiasm for the company and the opportunity that is up for grabs.

He knows there will be many applicants for the few openings available, and it is his responsibility to demonstrate why he is uniquely qualified to fill one of the openings. His ability as a salesman will be put to the test, and one of the basic purposes of the question is to discover how convincing the applicant can be in his answer.

The answer, whether from a college senior or a master's candidate, should cover all relevant areas:

1. Educational and work experience credentials.
2. Compatibility with applicant's career objectives.
3. Enthusiasm for the job and the company.
4. Eagerness to accept the challenges offered by the job.
5. Desire to succeed with the company and to make substantial contributions to it.

It is true that this is only a screening interview and that its basic purpose is to separate the wheat from the chaff. What will impress the interviewer? Possibly the most telling point an applicant can make is to get across his desire for the position. Blasé individuals don't get to first base. The interviewer has what is, to him, a good to offer—an attractive job—and he will be turned off if the applicant exhibits a "so what" attitude. He will be turned on if an applicant indicates that he wants the job so much he can taste it. If an applicant is truly enthusiastic about an opening, his enthusiasm will show in his words, his actions, and his manner.

Of course, this is not a vaudeville show, and the applicant should not be putting on an act, however well rehearsed. But, if the job is what you are truly looking for, let the interviewer know how you feel. Don't be ashamed to show your excitement.

Yet, don't turn into a con man and try to outsmart the interviewer. If you go into ecstasies over the Kokomo sanitation department opening in which your badge of honor will be a broom, you will be quickly labeled a phony—and rightly so.

Save your enthusiasm for what really excites you, and let it shine forth only then.

Let's try the question on Janet Lacy, a geology major about to graduate from college. It is asked by a recruiter from a major oil company that is heavily engaged in exploration and drilling operations. Janet is looking directly at her questioner as she answers.

I can think of a number of reasons why you should hire *me*, Mr. Rockefeller. First of all, I am a geology major and I have done extremely well in my course work. The electives I have taken in higher math will be a big plus on the job we have been discussing. I have spent two summers on field trips in the West, and my experiences have reinforced my interest in the work and convinced me that I can become a competent exploration geologist.

The position is exactly in line with my objectives. I want to start in the field—learn the business from the ground up—or perhaps I should say from the ground down. As time goes on, I want to graduate into the management and planning areas of exploration.

I have read everything I could find on your company, and I have talked to several professors in my department. What I have read and heard supports my conviction that you are a leader in the industry with a deserved reputation of being a good company to work for.

I realize the job will be demanding, but the rewards can be equally great. I intend to succeed in any work I undertake, and I am impressed by the opportunities that will be available as I advance in your organization.

To sum it all up, you should hire me because I am intelligent, highly motivated, and competent to do the work the job requires. I am sold on your company and the opportunity you are offering, and I am convinced that I can become a valuable asset to you. I guess what I am saying is, I want the job, and I know I can handle it.

Has Janet done a good job in selling herself? I think so. She has matched a need to a product and has shown a perfect fit. Her answer has not been short—it took several minutes to deliver, but how could the time have been spent to better advantage?

A master's candidate will take the same approach to the question, fitting his experience, academic qualifications, and personal inclinations to the situation as Janet has done.

Hints:

□ Be prepared for this question. It arises in a majority of interviews. Have your basic answer ready.

□ If the position really excites you, let your excitement show.

□ Don't put on an act if it is a "ho-hum" job. Phonies are easily spotted.

□ Remember that if a choice must be made between two candidates of equal qualifications, the call-back invitation will probably go to the applicant who indicates that he really wants the job.

The job

Question: Have you any questions about the job we are offering?

A no would indicate a lack of interest. Pulling a list of questions out of a pocket and going down the sheet item by item will convince the interviewer that you have studied the job description he sent to your placement office but may not impress him in other respects. This is a preliminary screening interview, a get-acquainted session, and an opportunity for each of you to learn as much as you can about the other. A question such as "How many people would be in the room with me?" is frivolous. So also would be a question on the length of the lunch period.

On the other hand, it would be appropriate to ask how much time would be spent working alone and how much would be spent in a group. It would also be appropriate to ask a question on the opportunities for meeting the public or employees in other departments. Questio..s on the specific work to be done are proper. Is decision-making responsibility connected with the job? How much computational work is involved as contrasted with analysis and planning? To what areas do graduates from the job usually go after serving an apprenticeship? How soon does the first promotion usually come? How soon can an employee expect to be given more decision-making responsibility?

These are excellent questions. They are relevant, and they indicate that the applicant is highly motivated, wants to succeed, and is looking well beyond the constraints of the entry job.

Hints:

□ Again, be prepared.

□ Don't ask trivial questions.

□ Frame your questions to indicate that you are looking to the future well beyond your first position.

□ Give evidence of your desire to succeed, to make a rewarding career for yourself, and at the same time to give your employer full value.

Grades

Question: Tell me about your grades; how good a student have you been?

If you are a real brain and have earned one academic honor after another, you will be delighted to answer this question. Unfortunately, your résumé will list these distinctions and in such a case the recruiter probably will not pose the question. It will usually be directed to applicants whose résumés are discreetly silent on the subject of grades.

Fortunately, a majority of students will be able to field the question with ease and confidence. A solid B average is nothing to be ashamed of, and even lower grades may not be a handicap, provided that extracurricular accomplishments explain and substitute for them. There is much to be gained from education other than high academic standing.

In the "Education" section of Chapter 6 you will find a lengthy discussion of grades and grade transcripts, so at this point we will confine ourselves to possible answers to the question as it might be asked during an interview.

A college senior with adequate grades might answer this way.

I have never had any academic difficulties. I'll admit I probably could have done better, especially in my first two years, when I was adjusting to college life, but my involvement in campus affairs and sports made heavy demands on my time. Grades were important to me, but I also profited from my extracurricular experiences.

The senior might, at this point, give an example or two of his achievements and what he learned from them. In short, he mentions his grades and then shows how his other accomplishments contributed to his education.

Suppose a student's grades were less than satisfactory—what can he say? How about this?

I'm afraid my grades have not been as good as they should have been, but . . .

What the student says next is the critical factor. What reasons can he give?

1. I started off on the wrong foot, and I have been struggling for the last two years to get my average up. My grades have improved each semester, and I expect my final term to be my best.

2. Because of family circumstances it has been necessary for me to earn a large portion of my college expenses. It has been a struggle, and I'm afraid my grades may have suffered somewhat. Yet, the effort has been worth it to me, and when I get my diploma in a few months I'm going to be proud of my accomplishment.

3. I was an excellent student in high school, and when I came to college, I'm afraid I didn't realize how much more demanding my course work would be. I involved myself in a number of activities, and although I enjoyed the work and learned much from it, my grades were affected. This year I have cut back my outside activities and am doing much better in the classroom.

4. My father is a doctor, and I always wanted to follow in his footsteps. I started in the premed program, and it took me two years to realize that I had neither the aptitude nor the desire to be a doctor. I switched to economics and had to do a lot of extra work to catch up. I'm glad I made the change and know what I want to do after I graduate. My grades suffered during the process of change, but I now feel comfortable and competent in my chosen field.

The central theme of the four answers is this:

1. Admit less than satisfactory performance.
2. Give reasons for it.
3. Show that you were aware of shortcomings.
4. Demonstrate how you have coped with the problem and profited from it.

Hints:

□ Don't attempt to gloss over poor grades.

□ Analyze the causes, and describe the remedies you have adopted.

□ Never blame poor grades on professors who don't like or appreciate you.

□ Don't give the impression that you feel you were unfairly treated and that your poor grades weren't really your fault.

□ Remember that your most recent grades are the most important ones. A good junior year and a better senior year will do much to compensate for poor performance earlier.

A candidate for a master's degree will have a slightly different approach to the question. Many graduate schools do not compute grade averages or class standings, and in such schools a student knows only how he has done and may be unaware of how he stands with respect to his classmates.

The master's candidate might phrase his answer this way.

I expect to receive my degree in June, and that will indicate my satisfactory completion of the program. I am content with my grades and feel that I am fully equipped to handle any job I might undertake.

If your path to a degree has not been free of stumbling blocks, you might respond like this.

I came to graduate school directly from college without the advantage of any full-time work experience. Everything was so different I floundered around for a while until I got on to the system and learned how to handle the heavy work load. This year I am much more confident of my ability and am doing well in my courses.

A student with 10 years' work experience might have encountered a related problem. Returning to academic life after such a long absence might have required an adjustment period. If this resulted in lower than expected grades in the first year, don't be reluctant to admit it. The second year should be a different story.

In general, receiving an advanced degree from an accredited institution should be ample evidence of scholastic competence. If, on your way to a degree, you encountered obstacles, don't be ashamed to admit them and show how you conquered them. The recruiter will understand and approve.

Hints:

□ Completion of the course and the expectation of receiving a degree should answer the grade question.

□ Rely on the expected degree and don't belabor the recruiter with a chronicle of individual course grades.

□ If you have received any academic awards in either college or graduate school, find a way to mention them even though the recruiter never brings up the issue of grades.

Illegal or improper questions

Up to now we have considered only questions an interviewer can ask with propriety. Many are good relevant questions; some are not; but all are the interviewer's prerogative to ask if he so desires. Other questions are improper because they are either illegal or offensive to good taste.

In an effort to end discrimination and enforce equal opportunity in employment the government has declared that many questions related to sex, race, color, creed, marital status, age, political affiliation, association memberships, and so forth, may not be asked. Yet, many questions on these subjects are frequently put to applicants, and not a few of them appear to be reasonable. For instance, I can see nothing wrong in asking a person how old he or she is and whether or not he or she is married. Both questions are improper. Indeed, if Mary Jones and Jim Thomas, hoping to buy a house, apply to a financial institution for a mortgage loan, the lending officer is not legally permitted to ask whether they are married or engaged or even contemplating such a momentous action.

Individuals often supply such vital statistics as age, weight, height, and marital status in a résumé, but if the information is not included, the interviewer is not allowed to request it. The moment of truth arrives after the individual has been employed and fills out health insurance and tax withholding forms.

If an applicant is asked an illegal question, what can or should he reply?

1. "That is an illegal question. I refuse to answer." (In other words, "It's none of your business.")
2. "You have violated the law. I'm going to report you to..."

(whoever or whatever is the proper government agency).
3. "You are not allowed to ask that question, but I am 22 years old."

None of these answers will endear you to the interviewer. Each of them is justified, but what will be the result? Like the unsuccessful salesman, you will have won the argument but lost the order.

Even worse would be this answer if you were asked whether you had ever been convicted for a crime or spent time in jail. "That is an illegal question. If you don't hire me for this job, I'll report you to the authorities." Your reply would be just as illegal as the question, and what do you think your chances for promotion would be if your blackmail attempt were effective?

Experienced recruiters are aware of what they can and cannot ask. Alas, not all interviewers are true professionals. So, specific rules cannot be designed to cover answers to every illegal or improper question that might be asked.

As a general rule, I see nothing wrong with a gracious reply to an improper question if the answer is not contrary to your principles or your interests.

Thus, when an interviewer asks a college senior, "How old are you, Linda?" why not answer, "I am 21"? It is an unnecessary question—granted. The interviewer has your résumé and knows you have gone straight through your schooling and are probably 21 or 22. What does the difference of a year make? So, why make a big deal of it?

On the other hand, suppose an interviewer notices that a woman is wearing an engagement ring and a wedding band and says, "I see you are married. Do you have children?"

Now, we are on a sticky wicket. If you have none, you might answer no. On the other hand, if you have a couple of youngsters running around the house, you might feel, and reasonably so, that mentioning the fact might lessen your chances of getting the job. The interviewer had no right to ask the question, but he did. If you really want the job, your answer must not be abrasive. You may wish to temporize. "At present I'd rather not go into personal issues. We can take them up when we are much closer to a decision on the position we are discussing."

Such an answer lets the interviewer know he is treading on shaky ground. At the same time it indicates your willingness to discuss the question when you are being seriously considered for the position.

If you are unmarried, you might answer a question on your status with, "I'm single." If the interviewer persists and asks whether you want to have children when you do get married, he is guilty on two counts. The question is both unlawful and an invasion of privacy. A good answer might be, "At present I have no plans in that direction."

Of course, if the interviewer is a complete and persistent boor, you wouldn't want to work for a company that would employ such an idiot and you may decide to terminate the interview and report the matter to the placement office so that it can make a complaint to the company.

Suppose you are a man and a college senior. The interviewer asks whether you are married. "No," you reply, "but I plan to get married this summer. Claire and I have decided that I should accept the best job opportunity that comes to me, and when I know where we will be living, she will look for a job there." I doubt whether such an answer would be offensive to your principles. Should the interviewer ask about your plans for a family, you might reply that you have not come to any conclusion on the matter with your fiancée. I would be surprised if the interviewer asked the second question after hearing your answer to the first. But, the world is full of surprises.

In general, I would say that women have more difficulty than men in fielding questions on marriage. Years ago few corporations would hire married women at all. Those were the days when a married woman's place was in the home and her highest aspiration was to have a good provider for a husband and a gaggle of children to rear. Times have changed, thank heaven, but problems do arise when interviewers are not as modern in their thinking as I am or as understanding of the changes in the world as it is today.

A word of warning. Some interviewers are capable of extraordinarily agile footwork when skating about the edges of illegal questions. They would never be guilty of making an improper request for information, but they may achieve the same result by posing a perfectly legal question and allowing the unwary applicant to dig his own grave if he has an inclination to do so.

"Are there any major issues that concern you at the present moment?" The recruiter displays a benign smile as he poses the question. An unwitting individual might respond like this. "Yes, I was a strong supporter of ERA and worked for several years in an effort to secure passage of the amendment in my home state."

The interviewer raises an inquiring eyebrow, and the applicant makes an impassioned argument for her beliefs. Who can blame the interviewer for his reaction?

I'm not saying it isn't an individual's privilege to feel strongly on a subject—that is his or her prerogative. It is, however, not always appropriate to express one's sentiments.

Another individual might respond, "I am alarmed by the inherent danger connected with the development of atomic power."

"That's interesting. What direction does your concern take?" Nothing illegal there.

Can the interviewer be faulted if the applicant recounts how he spent an uncomfortable night in the slammer after having been arrested during an illegal protest at a nearby reactor?

My advice? Keep a tight curb on your hobbyhorses. Let sleeping equines lie. There is a time and place for everything, and a job interview is not the proper occasion to mount your soapbox.

Keep away from inflammatory and controversial issues. Be concerned with the state of the economy, politics (if you must), foreign policy, and so forth, but don't take off on your pet peeves in an argumentative manner.

On the other hand, don't show a total lack of concern with what is going on in the world.

"I've got too many problems of my own to worry about what doesn't concern me." That would be a terrible answer—heartless, selfish.

"I try to stay abreast of current affairs, and, like everyone else, I am distressed with much of what I observe. I'd like to see more real interest in people, more concern with ethics and honesty, more statesmanship and less politics."

Superficial? Perhaps, but you are interviewing for a job. Field the question; escape the snare the recruiter may have deliberately set for you; and get back to the purpose of the meeting.

Hints:

□ Be prepared to handle illegal or improper questions.

□ If you are really interested in a job opportunity, don't refuse to answer a question that does not offend your principles.

□ Politely finesse a question that you do not wish to answer directly.

□ Keep your cool. Don't be a fool yourself simply because the interviewer is one. You know better, and he obviously doesn't.

□ Don't self-destruct. Avoid involvement with legal but potentially dangerous questions, and get back to establishing your qualifications for the job under discussion.

4

Screening interviews

Closing the interview

Let us suppose the interview has proceeded smoothly; you have developed a friendly relationship with the interviewer, questions have been asked and answered, and you have a good feel for the job opportunity you are discussing. The interviewer glances casually at his watch. You have been keeping an eye on your own, and you are aware that your half hour is nearly up. How should you wrap up the interview? If you're not impressed with the company or the opportunity, you really don't care, but if the interview has strengthened your conviction that this is the company you want to work for, the close can be extremely important to you.

Suppose Mr. Spencer rises, sticks out his hand, and says, "Thanks for stopping by, Jack. We'll be in touch." Do you take his hand, mutter, "Um, um, thanks," and beat an ignominious retreat? I would prefer that you say something like this:

I enjoyed our discussion, Mr. Spencer—you have been very helpful—and I am impressed with what you have told me about your company and the position you have to offer. I do hope I will have the opportunity for further discussions with ABC Corporation. Can you tell me how soon I can except to hear from you?

Nail it down. If you are truly interested, let the interviewer know it and don't let him kiss you off. Perhaps his casual remark was aimed at learning whether you were really interested in working for his company or just shopping. Make your feelings clear.

Should you respond as suggested, Mr. Spencer will probably smile, give your hand an additional shake, and say, "Glad to know you feel that way, Jack. You can count on hearing from me within two weeks." It is very unlikely that he will offer you a second interview on the spot, but the door is open and you have secured a commitment from him.

Having accomplished your purpose, you may now make way for the classmate who is waiting impatiently and apprehensively outside the door.

Hints:

□ Make sure the interview ends on a positive note. Don't let it dwindle away and go out with a whimper.

□ Ask for a specific time commitment for a response from the company.

□ Continue to sell until the very end of the interview.

□ Never allow the interviewer to doubt your interest in and desire for the job he has to offer.

Postinterview actions

The actual interview ends when you walk out of the room, but there is still much you must do before you tackle your next recruiter.

Your first chore is to make notes on the interview. This record is especially important if you have scheduled a number of interviews, since memory can be uncertain after the passage of time. Thus, your notes will cover the highlights of the interview: the personality of the interviewer, particulars of the job in question, company policies that impressed you, questions you think of after the conclusion of the interview. In addition, you will write a short analysis of how you handled the interview; what you did well, where you missed the boat, how you should improve your performance the next time.

As a part of your preparation for subsequent interviews you will review your notes on earlier ones. Your technique should improve with every interview.

You will make a note on your calendar of the date by which you expect to hear from the company. Let's talk about the calendar a bit.

Every individual who expects to be active in the job market should keep one. I recommend large sheets—one month to a sheet. You will need space to list all your scheduled interviews, showing company name and time of interview. You will make an entry for the date you expect to hear the results. If you are fortunate enough to be invited for an office visit, you enter the date as soon as it has been determined. After the trip you will make a note on the date when you expect to be told the outcome. When you receive an offer, you will be asked to respond by a certain time. That date should be entered, and you had better not forget to let the person know your decision promptly.

You will find that having a comprehensive record all in one place is essential if you are to keep all your ducks lined up. Nothing can be more damaging to your chances than a missed interview or a neglected commitment.

Finally, you write your thank-you letter. Your note is not only evidence of a good upbringing but is also an excellent selling medium. It is so important that we'll devote a section to it, and since there's no time like the present, we'll get right at it.

Thank-you letters

When grandma sends you a check for a graduation present, what is the first thing you do? The first thing, that is, after you convert the check to cash and pay off some nagging bills. You write her a friendly appreciative note to express your thanks. And, you better write it immediately, or it's two to one you'll never write it at all. Right?

Your response to a favorable interview should be exactly the same. A man or woman you have never seen before has spent half an hour with you finding out what kind of person you are and telling you about a company and the job opportunities it has to offer. He or she has been courteous and friendly. You would like to receive a job offer from the company, but for the moment there is not much you can do to further your candidacy. The thank-you note is your single opportunity to improve your chances for further consideration and a call-back interview.

Put yourself in the position of the interviewer. He has spent two days at your school and has talked to more than 20 of your classmates. He has a copy of your résumé and the notes he made during or after the interview, but 20 names and faces tend to blur a week later, just as your interviews will tend to blur after you have gone through 20 of them.

Now, suppose that four or five days after having been to your school, the interviewer receives a letter from you thanking him for his consideration and reiterating your interest in his company and the job he has to offer. Isn't it natural that he will be pleased with this evidence of interest and old-fashioned courtesy? Other things being equal, a small and simple act might tip the scales in your favor. The letter will be placed in your file, and your name will be fresh in the interviewer's mind when he makes his decision on who should be called in for a second round of talks.

So far, so good, but what about the letter itself? My first suggestion is that you write it on your school or college letterhead. Why? This supplies an immediate clue as to where the interview took place. Suppose you used the writing paper with your name and address printed at the top that Aunt Sarah gave you as a Christmas present. The address is in New York City, but last week the interviewer saw undergraduates at Columbia, NYU, Manhattan College, and City College and master's candidates at Columbia and NYU. You'll have to spend a sentence or two identifying yourself with the proper institution. On the other hand, if the name of your school or college is emblazoned across the top of the sheet, you avoid the identity difficulty.

Next point. The letter should be short and concise—no fancy frills or casual chitchat. Thank the interviewer, show interest in the job, remind him that you are waiting to hear from him, and stop right there. Don't mention the weather or the state of the union. What do you think of the sample on page 70?

Polite, short, not pushy but positive. I would say it is a good letter.

Let's take a look at the sample on page 71.

There are a number of things about this letter that displease me.

1. Don't write to *Dear Sir;* write to *Mr. Spencer,* the person with whom you talked for half an hour.
2. Proofread what you write. *Meeting* has two *e*'s and one *t; hnow* doesn't spell *know.*

HICKSVILLE COLLEGE
Hicksville, N.D.

January 25, 19XX

Mr. George Spencer
Employee Relations Department
XYZ Corporation
Skelton, Georgia 30303

Dear Mr. Spencer:

   I enjoyed our interview Tuesday afternoon and appreciate very much the time and consideration you gave me.

   I have a strong interest in XYZ Corporation and the employment opportunity we discussed. I feel I can make a substantial contribution to your company and look forward to hearing from you.

Sincerely,

David Hill

David Hill
2426 Arlington Boulevard
Hicksville, N.D. 60809

HICKSVILLE COLLEGE
Hicksville, N.D.

January 25, 19XX

Mr. George Spencer
Employee Relations Department
XYZ Corporation
Skelton, Georgia 30303

Dear Sir:

   I enjoyed metting with you this past Friday. I am very willing
to continue the discussion of the possibility of employment
with your company. If there is anything I can do to further my
employment application, please let me hnow.

Sincerely,

Thomas Glenn

3. You sound patronizing when you state that you are willing to continue discussions. Are you really doing XYZ a favor by applying to it for a job?
4. You don't remind Mr. Spencer that you expect to hear from him soon.
5. Signing your letter *Tom* is a little presumptuous. Even if Mr. Spencer called you by your first name during the interview, you should be more formal when you write him. Signing *Tom Glenn* would be satisfactory.
6. It is wise to show your address on the letter.

Now, let's look at one more bread and butter letter. This was written by a master's candidate with several years business experience and the opening was at a relatively high level.

This letter is longer than the other samples. The reason is that David is more experienced than the other two letter writers and that the job is at a higher level and requires technical knowledge. David takes the opportunity to do a bit of personal selling, and at the same time he doesn't miss the chance to comment favorably on company policies he approves. He also lets his enthusiasm for the job show clearly.

Given David's experience and his obvious interest in the job, I feel that this is an excellent letter.

Query: Should a follow-up letter be written after every interview? Let's be practical about it—some interviews never get off the ground. Personalities don't mesh, the job doesn't appeal to you, or it develops that the opening is at a 50-year-old plant situated a hundred miles from the closest city. The interviewer and you soon lost interest in each other. Why waste your time and his by writing a letter he will have to read?

On the other hand, if you are interested, let the interviewer know it.

COLONIAL UNIVERSITY
GRADUATE SCHOOL OF BUSINESS ADMINISTRATION

January 25, 19XX

Mr. George O'Neill
Plandome Corporation
165 Fifth Street
Baltimore, Maryland 21031

Dear Mr. O'Neill:

I enjoyed our meeting and appreciate your taking the time to talk to me at length. It pleased me that we covered so much in our interview.

I am excited about the prospect of becoming involved in the work you are doing. My training and knowledge of analytical techniques give me confidence that I have the ability to make an important contribution to your effort. In addition, I have the motivation and desire to excel in any assignment I undertake. An important factor in my enthusiasm is the understanding that while performance is a necessary ingredient for success at Plandome, the company regards as highly important the personal growth and professional integrity of its employees.

Again, I enjoyed our meeting and look forward to hearing from you.

Sincerely,

David Slope

David Slope
Route 5, Box 35F
Clinton, MD 20735

Hints:

□ Use a thank-you note as a follow-up to a successful interview.
□ Keep the note gracious, short, and to the point.
□ Include these elements:
  1. Thanks for your time.
  2. I am interested in the opportunity.
  3. I am impressed by what I have learned about your company.
  4. I look forward to hearing from you.

Entertainment by recruiters

As we have stated, many colleges and graduate schools compile a book containing résumés of students. The book is sold at a nominal price to potential employers that wish to purchase it. An index lists each student's fields of inerest: accounting, advertising, banking, computer application, management consulting, real estate, transportation, and so forth. A student might be listed in more than one category.

Prior to a campus visit, a recruiter who has studied the résumés of students expressing an interest in an area in which he has openings may write personal letters to some or all of them asking that they sign for an interview. He may even invite the group to a reception or dinner the evening before his interviewing schedule begins. He will also include on his list of invitees any student whom he knows personally or who has worked with his company as either a permanent employee or a summer intern.

Such affairs are frequently held at the hotel or motel where the company representatives are staying. The junior member of the group is usually charged with the responsibility for making the necessary arrangements, and if he wants to get ahead in his company, he had better do a good job. As a rule, only the more prestigious and affluent companies follow this route, but it has a lot to recommend it since it gives the corporate representatives an opportunity to meet prospective employees in a social environment.

In general, students are flattered and encouraged when they receive an invitation to such an affair. How should they handle themselves?

First of all, the invitation should be acknowledged promptly and either accepted or rejected. Few are refused—after all, who turns down an opportunity to drink and dine with congenial companions at no cost?

> Dear Mr. Spencer:
>
> I accept your invitation to dinner next Tuesday and am looking forward to meeting you and the members of your group before I interview with you Wednesday morning.
>
> Sincerely,
>
> Sally Long

The note is written on college or school stationery and is addressed to the person who issued the invitation.

Promptly at six o'clock Sally enters the Franklin Suite at the hotel and is greeted by Mr. Spencer. She introduces herself and is presented to the two other recruiters who accompany Mr. Spencer. A dozen classmates are already present, and the balance of the group arrives shortly after Sally. All are prompt, and all, like Sally, are well scrubbed and clad in their best bib and tucker.

Sally realizes that this is a purely social occasion and that her primary obligation is to be as pleasant as she can to her hosts. She will contrive to spend several minutes with each of the company representatives, and in her conversation with them she will not bring up anything connected with her career plans or the jobs the company has to offer even though she has reviewed her information on the company and its job openings. Such matters will be covered in her interview the next day. She will not—repeat, not—spend her time in a corner chatting with classmates.

Mr. Spencer or one of his minions will escort Sally to the bar to see that she gets the drink of her choice. It might be a beer, a glass of wine, or a highball. If she prefers, Sally can ask for a soft drink or mineral water, but there is no reason to deny herself the pleasure of an alcoholic beverage should she desire one. However, if that is her choice, she would be wise to restrict her consumption to a single drink—not that two or even three would make her tipsy—because, in the eyes of recruiters, moderation is a virtue. Besides, wine will probably be served at dinner, and Sally, again, will drink with discretion.

At dinner Sally finds herself at Mr. Genster's table. The conversation will be animated, covering such topics as the university basketball team, Near Eastern politics, and the president's plans for balancing the budget. Sally was an economics major in college, and she has strong feelings on several of the issues discussed. Yet, she does not attempt to dominate the conversation; when she has something to say, she says it, and then she quietly listens while others talk.

Before leaving, Sally thanks Mr. Spencer and his associates for a pleasant evening. When she meets Mr. Genster in the interview room the next morning, she doesn't forget to thank him again for his company's hospitality.

So much for Sally. What have Mr. Spencer and his fellow recruiters been up to during the party? They, too, have been enjoying themselves, but they have been working at the same time—observing social graces, manners, personalities. Who talks well? Who talks too much, too little? Who is relaxed and at ease? Who appears to be uncomfortable in the environment? Who knew or didn't know how to dress? Did anyone drink excessively?

After the party is over, the recruiters will spend a half hour comparing impressions of the students they have entertained. The selection process has already begun although interviews have not yet started.

Hints:

☐ Acknowledge an invitation immediately.

☐ Be on your best behavior—act like a lady or a gentleman.

☐ Be discreet in your drinking.

☐ Put your best foot forward—dress, manner, courtesy.

☐ Make sure you spend time with each company representative.

☐ Be sure to talk, but spend more time listening.

☐ Thank each of the recruiters for a pleasant evening.

Many companies do not put on a spread such as we have described but do meet interested students the evening before interviewing starts. A notice will be posted on the bulletin board stating that a classroom has been reserved and that company representatives will make a presentation on the company and the opportunities it offers graduating students. At the end of the presentation they will ask for and answer questions. Finally, beer, coffee, and snacks will be provided.

Attending students should dress and act in the same way as they would at a dinner meeting, but since the subject of available jobs has been introduced, questions on this subject are proper.

During the refreshment period a wise student will make his or her good manners perceptible to each recruiter and will not neglect to thank each of them for the information and the hospitality.

Meetings such as we have discussed are more usual at graduate schools than at colleges, but student deportment at either graduate schools or colleges should be of the same high quality.

Both types of meetings give the student the chance to display his wares in their best light. He should not fail to take advantage of every selling opportunity offered him.

Special problems of couples

The number of families with two wage earners has increased at an astounding rate in recent years. There are two major reasons for this phenomenon. Rises in prices have outstripped wage increases to the point that in many cases a single jobholder is unable to support a family on his pay alone. In addition, many women have decided that life should offer more than what the role of housewife affords. These are both compelling reasons, and the second is mainly responsible for the enrollment of large numbers of women in graduate programs other than the ones traditionally dominated by women, such as education and nursing. Nearly a third of the students seeking an MBA are now women, and many of these women are either married at the time of their graduation or achieve the state of bliss shortly thereafter.

Complications arise when a couple enter the job hunt simultaneously. If the groom accepts a job in Los Angeles and the bride begins her business career in Boston, the union might well be a barren one unless the spouses arrange to meet on occasion at or near McCook, Nebraska. Such a solution is not recommended; the costs would be prohibitive, and it would defeat the whole purpose of marriage.

A situation such as the one described, while not without precedent, is, I am happy to say, quite unusual. Most spouses do find a way to get jobs within living distance of each other. I know a young couple, both spouses with an MBA, who live in a small town on the Indiana-Ohio border. Each morning he points his car westward and drives 20 miles to his Indiana factory while she drives 22 miles east to her office at a company headquartered in Ohio. Finding those two jobs so close together was not easy.

How does a couple cope with the problem? I should think that the husband and wife would plan their job hunting strategy very carefully: decide in what area or areas they would prefer to make their home and construct their interview schedules based on these preferences. Should New York be a selected spot, and should the wife, looking for a banking job, receive an excellent offer from Chase Manhattan and her husband, looking for a position in brand management, receive an offer from General Foods in White Plains, all would be rosy. If they wanted country living, they could reside in Westchester County or lower Connecticut. She could commute by train to the big city, and he could drive to work. If they preferred the glamour of New York, she could walk to work or use the bus and he could commute against the grain.

Suppose, however, that his offer was not from General Foods but from Procter & Gamble in Cincinnati. I would hope that he would attempt to secure an offer from a company in New York while she would immediately institute a campaign directed at financial institutions in Cincinnati. They might even decide to make a concerted effort in Minneapolis. General Mills is a high-ranking company, and there are many fine banks in the twin cities of Minneapolis and St. Paul.

Make no mistake about it. It is difficult enough for a single person to find the job he wants. When there are two people to be satisfied, the attendant problems, to coin a phrase, take a quantum leap.

Complications arise when an offer is made to one person and he or she is unable to give a definite answer because the other has no present prospects in the area. Recruiters are aware of the difficulties encountered by couples and are usually generous in allowing time for ultimate decisions. At times they will even attempt to assist the spouse in finding opportunities in the area.

Yet, despite the exercise of all the goodwill in the world and despite conscientious efforts to find an acceptable solution, an impasse may occur. He has a fine offer in Chicago; she can take the job of her dreams in Boston. Neither has been able to find anything suitable in the other city or in mutually acceptable alternative locations. What happens?

No problem exists if the jobs are more important than the marriage. He goes his way; she goes hers. That is a shocking solution, but it is not unheard of. I don't feel as bad as I should about such an outcome; no marriage based on such a selfish attitude could long endure under any circumstances.

A well-married couple will ultimately reach the conclusion that one or the other must give way. The question is, Which? This is a hairy dilemma. There are no immutable laws that serve as certain guides; no historic precedents have achieved universal acceptance. On top of this, who is qualified or even presumptuous enough to assume the right to tell married couples how to order their lives? Having said all that, I'll now give you the opinion of one man.

It seems to me that there can never be an absolutely equal relationship in a marriage just as there can never be an absolutely equal relationship in a business partnership. One or the other partner must dominate, or the partnership will dissolve the first time the principals find themselves diametrically opposed on a major issue. I am not saying that one marriage or business partner should dominate the other on all decisions. People of goodwill can usually find a way to decide the normal sticky issues that plague any close relationship. One partner gets his way on one occasion, the other on a later one.

But then a major issue may erupt, and the best solution may not be to decide it in favor of the spouse whose turn it is to call the shot. Take this situation, for example. Both spouses have excellent jobs in the Boston area, and both are dedicated to their professional careers. The husband is asked by his company to transfer to a division headquarters in Atlanta. It is a tremendous opportunity which can lead to a high executive post in a few years. Refusing the offer would do substantial damage to the possibility of achieving the husband's career plan. Accepting the offer, however, would force his wife to resign her position and seek less rewarding work in Atlanta. Last summer she would have preferred to spend their vacation in the White Mountains of New Hampshire. Yet he preferred a house at the Jersey shore and she yielded to his wishes.

Now it's her turn to be gratified, but the decision is too important to be decided in such a manner.

Take another situation. Two students will marry shortly after receiving their MBA degrees. For four months they have frantically attempted to secure jobs in the same city. Finally, their efforts have met with success. Both students receive offers from firms in Richmond. The positions offered aren't the greatest opportunities in the world, but the couple will be together, and that is important to them. A few days before they are scheduled to announce their acceptances, the man receives an offer to be assistant to the president of a medium-size company in Charlotte, North Carolina. It is just the job he has been dreaming of. The pay is high, the responsibilities are great, and the prospects for advancement are excellent. If he accepts the offer, his fiancée will be left high and dry. She'll have to start looking all over again, with no assurance of finding any job commensurate with her qualifications.

Turn it around. What if the woman had been offered the Charlotte opportunity? Making a decision based on whose turn it is or on the toss of a coin won't do.

One more example, and then we'll consider a possible basis for making decisions of this type.

A couple were employed by a large retail store. Both held excellent positions: he in the administrative area and she as a buyer who had established an enviable reputation in her field. Early each morning they drove 40 or 50 miles to the store, and they returned late in the evening. Saturdays were regular workdays for both. Their three young children were adequately cared for by domestic help, but it was obvious that the children saw little of their parents and that family relations were not as close as they might have been. The husband was disenchanted with his job, while his wife reveled in the controlled chaos in which she functioned.

The husband resigned, ran the house, chauffeured the children, and, in effect, became the family homemaker, while the wife supported the ménage on her earnings alone. He was supremely happy in his new role—and it was a necessary one—while she continued to do what she loved and was enormously talented in doing. Everyone benefited from the change. I'm not sure what the moral is, but the solution certainly worked.

Now I'll try to draw a few conclusions from my ramblings. Let's start with a generalization. It seems to me that any organization needs one big boss—someone who calls the shots when the other executives are unable to reach agreement on a problem. Responsibility for the outcome of a battle rests with the ranking general. The president is accountable for the actions of his administration. Similarly, either the husband or the wife must be in a position to make a binding decision if there is a disagreement on a major issue. In years gone by, the husband normally, and as a matter of historic right, assumed this authority. And why not? He was the breadwinner, the head of the household, and without him the family would be destitute.

Now, however, things are different. Many times the wife earns more than her husband, has equal or superior capability, and may be more strongly motivated. Why shouldn't such a woman assume the top spot? I see no reason why she shouldn't. Yet, such instances are the exception rather than the rule. Many women of considerable talent and well-defined goals do not intend to make a lifetime career of their profession. These women intend to delay having children for a few years, and during that time they work diligently to help establish a base for the family fortune. When the husband is well on the road to success and the children are growing, the wife intends to enter on a new career—that of mother and homemaker. Her present career is important to her, but she can look ahead to the time when the family's prosperity will depend on the efforts of her husband.

In such a case I feel that the wife should defer to the interests of her husband in deciding which of them should be gratified in accepting a job offer. In the long run his business career will be more important to the family than hers; consequently, job decisions even early in the marriage should favor the husband.

At the same time it would not do for the husband to assume that the wife will automatically approve his actions and that it is therefore not necessary for him to discuss them with her. If she concurs in his approach to the issue, all will be well; if she is unwilling to delegate top-authority decisions to him, problems will ensue.

Married or about-to-be-married couples should reach some

type of understanding on this subject long before they start looking for jobs. Each person should appreciate the needs and desires of the other person and should be as unselfish and compromising as possible.

It is time for another digression before I conclude this section. I have reread many times what I have written in an effort to determine whether I might have ruffled the sensitivities of some readers. I sincerely hope not, for nothing could be farther from my intention. What I have attempted to do is to point out problem areas that may be encountered by job hunting couples and to suggest a basis for solving them. Feel free to disagree with what I have said—draw your own conclusions, make your own decisions, and more power to you. If you are content with your solution, I endorse it heartily. My sole purpose has been to point out potential complications in the hope that you will be prepared for them if they arise.

Hints:

- Discuss the issue and reach a decision before the job search starts.
- Keep the other person in mind when planning interviews.
- Realize that one partner or the other will probably have to use means other than the interview process at school in order to find a job.
- Remember also: Where there is a will, there is a way. Rational people with a deep concern for each other can find a mutually satisfactory solution to any problem that confronts them.

5

Follow-up interviews— Company trips

Now we'll explore the best of all possible worlds—the invitation to visit the home office of a company and meet a number of its executives. Let us suppose that sometime back you had what you thought was an excellent interview with Mr. Spencer of Mammoth Energy Corporation. At the close of the interview he promised to be in touch with you in about two weeks. You duly wrote your thank-you note, made an entry on your calendar so you wouldn't forget when you should hear from him, and returned to your daily grind of classes, preparation, and interviews.

Invitation to an office visit

Thirteen days later you were delighted to receive a letter from Mr. Spencer. The body of it read like this:

85

Dear Mary:

I would like very much to have you visit our home office in Houston at our expense. You will have the opportunity to meet other members of our organization, and we can continue our discussion of the possibilities of your joining our company.

Please call me collect at [telephone number] so we can make arrangements for your trip.

Sincerely,

George Spencer

You feel great; life is worthwhile, and even though it is sleeting outside, it is a beautiful day. Your first action should not be to grab the phone and place your call. You've got to think a bit first. Houston is a long way from where you are, and you can't just take off from classes at a moment's notice. Spring break comes at the end of the month—that would be an ideal time for the trip. You might even call the airport and find what connections can be made for Houston. You will also reread your notes on the interview and refresh your memory on Mammoth itself. Finally, you will list the items you want to settle with Mr. Spencer. Your list might look like this:

1. Thanks for the letter. (Don't forget this.)
2. Best time for me. (Write out the dates. Don't take the chance of getting confused on them.)
3. How do you prefer to handle airline tickets and expenses? (Have a record of flight schedules going and coming.)
4. Thanks again, I'm looking forward to seeing you.

Let's talk a little more about items 2 and 3. Mr. Spencer knows that your time is not entirely your own. You also realize that he works to a schedule. He may have allocated a week to the candidates he is inviting to Houston, and your appointment may have to be scheduled during that period. Don't offer just a single date; give him a choice. Of course, if only a single day is suitable to him, you may encounter a problem if it conflicts with a midterm exam or another interview. Companies, however, realize that such problems do arise and are usually accommodating in this respect.

A few words on expenses will suffice here since a section at the end of the chapter is devoted to this important topic. You are aware of your bank balance—a modest $36.27—and the air fare will amount to 5 or 10 times that amount. Mr. Spencer will be equally aware of your situation and will be quick to allay your fears by telling you how the cost of your trip will be handled without calling on your limited resources. Yet, in case he forgets to mention the matter, your list will remind you to bring it up.

So far, so good. Having prepared yourself, you take a deep breath and place your call to Mr. Spencer.

Good afternoon, Mr. Spencer. This is Mary Fisk at Bolton College. You asked me to call you about visiting your office.

A good start. You identified yourself, your school, and the purpose of your call. Next, you thank ᴍr. Spencer for his invitation and start discussing the particulars of the visit.

Since Mr. Spencer is an experienced interviewer, he will probably bring up most of the points we have mentioned, but your list will remind you if anything is overlooked. You will make a good impression if you have already checked air schedules and can offer flight numbers and times, both going and returning, so that tickets can be purchased and sent to you.

Hints:

- Show that you are prepared and can think things through.
- You are still selling—your organization skills and your ability to plan in advance.

Mr. Spencer seems to be pleased to have heard from you so promptly. People who are really interested don't put off the call for several days. Within a week you receive a friendly note from his secretary enclosing plane tickets, a reservation card at a downtown hotel, and information on transportation to the hotel and from it to the office. You are asked to arrive at the office at nine in the morning and to be prepared to spend the day there.

Conduct during office visit

At the appointed hour you present yourself at the reception desk of the Mammoth office. Your trip so far has been pleasant; the bus that took you to your hotel was just where you had been told it would be and your room was attractive. You enjoyed your dinner, and you took even greater pleasure in writing Mammoth's name on the bill above your signature. You were up early this morning, had breakfast, and returned to your room to make sure your grooming was perfect.

At the cashier's window you checked and signed your bill, and then accompanied by your suitcase, you took a cab to the office. Your return flight was scheduled for late afternoon, and you would leave for the airport directly from Mammoth.

At twenty seconds to nine the receptionist smiles up at you and says, "Good morning."

Good morning. I'm Mary Fisk. I have an appointment with Mr. Spencer.

Oh, yes. He told me you would be in this morning. Did you have a good trip? You are to go right in. I'll call his secretary, and she'll come for you.

Let's stop right here for a minute and analyze what is happening. Mary's mind is working at full speed. Her antennae are alertly picking up all kinds of signals. The reception room is large, and it is comfortably furnished in excellent taste. Mammoth has plenty of money and knows how to spend it. The receptionist is attractive, and she has an engaging smile and a pleasant manner. She appears to enjoy her job. Mary's arrival was expected. Arrangements had been made ahead of time. If Mary is astute, and I am sure she is, her respect for Mammoth will jump several notches. Her first impression is that Mammoth might be a good company to work for.

Her antennae will continue to soak up impressions all day long. Are the offices she sees well maintained? How are they furnished? Do the people she meets seem relaxed, or do most of them give the impression of being tense and under constant pressure? When she encounters people in a corridor, do they smile at her or do they hurry by with lowered heads? When she is passed from one person to another, do the two appear to be friends with an easy relationship, or do they seem to be carrying chips on their shoulders?

A safecracker would call it casing the joint, and Mary should be doing just that. Office environment can affect the desirability of a job to a great extent. Mary is constantly asking herself, "Can I be happy here—would I enjoy working here?"

Now, back to our muttons, as the French say. Mary is escorted to Mr. Spencer's office by his secretary. As they walk, Mary thanks her for the arrangements she made. Mr. Spencer greets Mary with a smile, chats with her for a minute or two, and gets down to business. A schedule has been set up. Mary will spend a half hour with him, and then she will be taken on a round of visits to meet other men and women in the organization, among them the three heads of the section where she would work if she joins the Mammoth organization. It will be a full day, broken only by lunch with several people in the executive dining room. Mary smiles a bit ruefully when she realizes that this lofty chamber will not again be open to her for a number of years if she comes to work for Mammoth.

It suddenly occurs to Mary that the company is doing a selling job on her and she is not the only salesperson present. She is putting her best foot forward, and so is the company.

Having outlined the day's schedule, Mr. Spencer asks, "Have you any questions for me?"

"First of all, would you go over the names and titles of the people I'll be seeing. I'd like to be sure I get them straight." Mary takes a pen and a small notebook from her purse and writes down the information. It will be important to her when she meets these people to know who and what they are.

Let us now digress for a while and spend some time on the psychology of the situation.

We have already discussed the relationship involved during the first interview at college. At that time Mary's objective was to pass the first hurdle, the screening interview. There were certain questions that she and the interviewer could ask and answer, and other questions that were inappropriate. The invitation to visit Houston demonstrated that Mary had passed her first test with flying colors. She is now at Mammoth's office at its invitation. The company must be interested in her as a prospective employee, or she would not have been invited. True, for every opening three or four or even more applicants may have been extended an invitation, but this does not affect the fact that Mary is among the chosen and that the company will attempt to convince her of Mammoth's desirability as an employer even though ultimately she may not be offered a position.

Appropriate questions

Thus, there has been a subtle change in roles. It is important that Mary put her best foot forward, but the company is on its best behavior as well. Mary can now seek answers to many questions it was inappropriate for her to pose in the first interview. Among the areas in which Mary might ask for information are:

1. Company policies on benefits such as life and health insurance.
2. Retirement plans.
3. Training programs.
4. Promotion policies.
5. Company plans for the future.
6. Projected expansion or contraction in particular areas.
7. Possible effects of competition or government regulations in the future.
8. Estimated profits over the next few years.

It would not have been fitting for Mary to question Mr. Spencer along these lines in the first interview, but it is now proper for her to do so. The situation has changed, and Mary's interest in these matters shows that she is not only intelligent but also seriously interested in the company.

You will note that Mary will mention nothing concerning vacation policy or compensation. There is plenty of time for those at the right moment, and that moment has not yet arrived.

Mr. Spencer, too, will have questions to ask. He has had time to restudy Mary's résumé and to review his notes on the preliminary interview. He might even ask several of the tough questions we have already discussed that he did not bring up in the first meeting.

Forty minutes later Mr. Spencer looks at his watch, rises, and says: "We'll start off in the Personnel Department. Ted Zimmerman will be waiting for you. He'll pass you on to Frank Moore, the head of the department where you might be working."

For the rest of the day Mary will be on the jump. By late afternoon she'll feel as if she has been through the wringer and she will be exhausted, emotionally and physically. It's tough being on your best behavior for a whole day, meeting one stranger after another and trying to make a good impression on each of them.

She was glad she had met Frank Moore when she was relatively fresh. He was vice president of the Planning Department, and he had two openings. He had spent half an hour with her, explaining the function of the department and outlining the responsibilities of the position for which she was a candidate. Mary was well prepared for this meeting. When the opportunity arose, she was ready with a number of questions.

If she joined the department, how much of her time would be spent working with others and how much of her time would she be on her own? What decision-making responsibility would she be given, and how soon? Should her work prove satisfactory, when could she expect to be given a promotion? What avenues would be open to her as she advanced through the department? Would there be an opportunity for transfer to a line job?

On this occasion none of these is a presumptuous question. These are questions that any potential employee with self-confidence and a desire to succeed might be expected to ask. Mr. Moore did not seem to be surprised by them, and he answered without quibbling, pointing out as he did so that everyone in the department was intelligent and well qualified, with the result that competition for advancement was strong. He also mentioned that Mammoth, because of its size, offered many opportunities for competent employees.

After her interview with Mr. Moore, Mary talked until lunch with his two assistants, who supervised the operation of the department. With these men, too, Mary was open, asking questions freely. She was particularly interested in the individuals in the department. What was their educational background? How long had they been in the department? When members of the department transferred out, where did they go? What was the attrition rate in the first two or three years of employment? If employees left, was there any common reason for their leaving?

Mary realized that she should not ask personal questions of these men, such as "How do they treat you here?" "What kind of a boss is Mr. Moore?" "Do you expect to stay here, or are you looking for another job?" Mary would have loved to get answers to these questions, but she had to assume that both men were loyal company employees and that they were very likely to report such questions to the boss when he asked them for their reactions toward Mary after their meeting with her.

A little before three o'clock Mary was led back to Mr. Spencer's office. She was tired, and she sat in a comfortable chair with a feeling of relief. Mr. Spencer smiled at her—he knew exactly how she felt.

"Well, Mary," he said, "what do you think of our shop?"

"It's great, Mr. Spencer, just great. Everyone was so nice to me; I got answers to every question I asked, and I must have asked a million. I was impressed with the people I met. Each of them seemed to like his job and, as far as I could tell, knew everything there was to be known about it. Mammoth is a very well-run company."

"I'm glad to hear you say that. All of us are proud of our company. I have already talked with several of the people you met. They seem to like you."

Mary smiles. "Thank you."

Fellow alumni

"Anything else you want to know, Mary?"

"No, but I wonder . . . I checked the alumni directory at school and found that two graduates work here. I don't know either of them—they were a bit before my time—but if possible I'd like to pay my respects to them."

"Certainly. Who are they?"

Mary has made another smart move. Graduates of an institution have something in common and are interested in each other. Spending a few minutes with each of the two graduates is a friendly gesture that may be helpful to Mary should she ultimately receive and accept an offer from Mammoth. She will have a couple of friends in court, and if her brief meeting strikes a chord of mutual interest, she may be able to seek advice on a personal basis if some issue arises in her later negotiations with the company on the job opening. All of Mary's other relationships with company people have been purely business ones, and an insider's suggestions and advice might be helpful to her.

Another short digression. I certainly don't want to leave the impression that everything an applicant does has an ulterior motive and that Mary is nothing but an unscrupulous Machiavelli, cynically pulling every string to con the opposition. Nothing could be farther from the truth. Mary is a very decent person, engaged for the first time in a job hunt, an endeavor in which she is totally inexperienced. What I am trying to do is, first of all, to explain the basic moves involved and then to suggest reasonable and ethical actions that Mary might take to better her position. It probably never entered Mary's head to inquire about other graduates of her college, and I mention this possibility only because I am sure that once such a move is suggested, she will immediately agree that it is a gracious action and she will genuinely want to make the acquaintance of fellow alumni. Graduates of business schools will find alumni in positions of high rank in many of the companies with which they interview. Such alumni can be and usually are of great help to candidates from their old school.

The same theory holds true for many of the other suggestions I have made. Why answer a question with a simple yes or no when making a more complete response will be more satisfactory to the questioner and at the same time will advance the candidacy of the applicant? Certainly, there is nothing unscrupulous or unethical in such an action. A top-flight tennis player seeks the best professional help he can find if he wishes to improve his game still further. Why shouldn't a job hunter do the same thing? Provided, of course, the applicant is actually being honest with himself and the interviewer. To deliberately misrepresent in order to gain an advantage is unethical and totally unacceptable. Honesty is a must if a lasting relationship is to be established. I hope I make myself clear on these points. Now, let's get back to Mary.

Outcomes of final meeting

What happens toward the end of her final meeting with Mr. Spencer? There are at least four possibilities.

1. Mr. Spencer says, "Mary, I'm sorry, but the job we have to offer does not appear to be suited to you. You do have

a lot going for you, and I am sure you will soon find the right opportunity."

In such an unlikely event the only response Mary can make is, "Thank you anyway, Mr. Spencer. You have been very kind to me, and I'm sorry it didn't work out. You have a wonderful company. If an opening more suitable for me occurs, please keep me in mind."

2. Mr. Spencer says: "We've enjoyed having you here, Mary. As you know, we are calling in several other applicants, and after we have had a chance to look at all of them, I'll be in touch with you."

Mary answers, "That's fine, Mr. Spencer. Thank you very much. Can you give me any idea when I might expect to hear from you?"

Hint:

□ Nail it down. Don't let it hang in midair. If you don't get word by the stated date, don't be reluctant to phone a day or two later. A call would be another indication of your interest and concern.

Let us suppose that the day had not gone well for Mary. She did not feel comfortable in the environment of the office, and she was not at ease during her meetings. The atmosphere had been cold and unfriendly. By lunchtime Mary had come to the decision that Mammoth was not the place for her even if she were offered a job. What should she do?

It wouldn't make sense for Mary to keep Mr. Spencer on the hook, nor would it be ethical for her to keep her decision to herself. Thus, in her final meeting with Mr. Spencer she might say, "You have been awfully nice to me, but I'm afraid I don't think it would be right for either of us if I worked here. I'm sorry I put you to the expense of bringing me here, but I feel that I must be honest with you."

Companies are forced to turn down many applicants, and they are aware that some candidates will turn them down. This is a fact of life, and it saves time and money as well as embarrassment later to speak openly once your mind is made up. The company will not dillydally if it decides that you will not fit into it, nor should you if you decide the job is not for you.

Hint:

□ Be polite, but don't fail to make your decision clear.

Suppose Mr. Spencer says, "I'm sorry you feel that way, Mary. Do you mind telling me why you made your decision?"

Tell him, but make your answer as objective as you can. Don't tell him that one of the men made a pass at you during an interview or that when you talked to the graduates of your school, both of them told you they intended to quit their jobs because they couldn't tolerate the viciousness of company politics.

Hint:

□ Retire gracefully. Don't stir up a hornet's nest. The interviewer can read between the lines. Don't spell it out for him with all the gory details.

3. Mr. Spencer says, "Mary, I've had a chance to talk to most of the people you saw today. All them were impressed with your credentials and especially with how well you handled yourself. In about 10 days I'm going to write you making you an offer. What do you think about that?"

Mary will probably bounce out of her chair and blurt out, "That's wonderful news. Thank you so much."

98

Hint:

☐ Mary does not say, "That's great. What salary will you offer me?" Unless Mr. Spencer mentions pay, Mary should say nothing about it. This is not a subject for Mary to mention. The written offer will contain the figure. Don't forget this point. Take it easy; don't push.

Of course, if Mary has already decided that Mammoth is not for her and Mr. Spencer makes the offer before she can tell him her decision, it will be more difficult for her to tell him how she feels. If she is positive that her decision is the right one, she should make it known; if she is not absolutely convinced that she does not want to work for Mammoth, it would not be improper for her to await the receipt of the offer before making her final decision.

Hint:

☐ If you are not positive of your feelings, don't burn your bridges behind you. Wait, and see what happens. There is nothing wrong with such an action.

4. Suppose Mr. Spencer says, "Mary, you've passed all your tests with flying colors, and I'm offering you the job at a starting salary of $_____. How does that sound to you?"

No one could really blame Mary if she ejaculated, "Wonderful—I accept," but I wouldn't recommend such a reaction. First of all, Mary should consider her feelings about working for Mammoth. We have already discussed what she might say if she were doubtful about accepting a position with the company. However, if she has been favorably impressed by the company and by the individuals she has met and she has no reservation about working for Mammoth, she might reply this way:

That's wonderful news. Thank you. I hope you can understand my position. As I have told you, I have interviewed with several companies and I expect to make other plant trips. I really feel I owe it to myself to explore every avenue open to me before I make my final decision. Of course, I am flattered by the offer and I am impressed by your company, but I hope you will give me time to weigh your offer against others I may receive.

In the Chapter 3 discussion of tough questions that an interviewer might ask during a screening session, we took up salary at considerable length. We stated that we did not consider discussion of this subject proper in a first interview. Now, however, the situation is different. It is not usual for a job offer to be made during a plant trip, but this does happen, and an applicant must be prepared for the possibility. It is entirely proper for the interviewer to bring up the question of salary, although I would still not recommend that the applicant broach the subject.

Recruiters realize that they are operating in a competitive market. Companies other than their own are also looking for qualified new employees. If an extremely attractive candidate presents himself, a company might make an offer early on in an attempt to secure a commitment ahead of competing organizations. On the other hand, the recruiting process is a lengthy one and no company wants to fill its quota of recruits before it has been able to evaluate the whole crop of candidates.

Candidates, too, should not be too hasty in accepting an early offer. They shouldn't commit themselves before investigating all the opportunities available to them.

Thus, I recommend caution in accepting unexpectedly quick offers. Most experienced recruiters understand the dilemma of applicants: it is the old bird-in-the-hand situation. They realize, however, that an applicant is entitled to an opportunity to survey the market, and they are prepared for a candidate's request for adequate time before giving a definite answer.

Having said this, I'll hedge a bit. It occasionally happens that something like love at first sight occurs between an individual and a corporation. The chemistry between Mary and Mr. Spencer may have been perfect. She may have been strongly attracted by every person she had seen all day. The research she had done on Mammoth may have convinced her that it was the number one company to work for in the country. The job as described to her may have been exactly what she had dreamed of getting. Perhaps she had friends in Houston who had told her it was a great place to live. The salary offered may have been far superior to the other offers she and her classmates had received.

In such an event, why delay acceptance? Who could fault Mary if she took the job on the spot? Certainly not I as long as I knew that Mary's decision was based on reason, not whim.

Hint:

□ Take your time—don't jump the gun. No important decision should have to be made at the drop of a hat.

Expenses incurred during office visits

Expenses and airline tickets are items that must be settled early on. Many of the larger companies have well-established policies to cover them. Furthermore, companies realize that with few exceptions students do not possess unlimited financial resources. Consequently, companies often offer to purchase the tickets and send them to the applicant. They will also make hotel or motel reservations and have the bill submitted directly to them. Some companies offer an expense advance to cover miscellaneous items such as meals and taxi or bus fares. If you are destitute, do not hesitate to accept such an offer, but if you can handle these expenses, do so and submit a statement after you return home. Many school placement offices make short-term loans to students to cover trip expenses that will not be reimbursed until later.

It is likely that expense forms along with instructions on how to complete them will be mailed to the applicant together with his tickets. If not, the reporting method should be settled during the visit so there is no question as to how expenses are to be handled and documented.

Companies can exert control by paying airline fares and lodging expenses directly. If they supply the tickets, they are assured that an applicant carried away by his own importance will not decide to travel first class and engage a suite at the airport motel.

An applicant should act conservatively with respect to expenses. Not niggardly, but with discretion. Don't take a cab to or from the airport when a bus will take you to the same destination at a fifth the cost. If you are accustomed to a full breakfast, have one, but that doesn't mean you must order orange juice, casaba melon, cereal, eggs, and bacon with side orders of ham and grits before you start on your coffee. Corporations can learn a lot about an individual from a study of his expense account. Suppose the company has arranged to have the hotel bill it directly and you casually charge four before-dinner drinks and then sign for three postprandial brandies. Eyebrows and probably tempers will rise when the bill is checked before payment. On the other hand, although a single drink before dinner would not be considered at all out of order, I think I might pay for my own drinks when traveling at company expense—at least until I was on the payroll. Likewise, a modest sirloin steak is priced more economically than Chateaubriand.

Hints:

- Treat yourself right, but don't act like an Arabian oil potentate.
- Remember that Mr. Spencer has seen dozens, perhaps hundreds, of expense accounts and that he knows how they can give insights into character.
- Whenever possible, secure receipts for expenditures not charged directly to the company. You will attach them to your expense account.
- If expense reporting forms have not been given to you, ask for them during your visit.
- Never fail to settle how expenses will be handled. Avoid future misunderstandings. Their result could be traumatic.

Expenses of multipurpose trips

A complication arises when an applicant visits more than one company on a single trip. Let us say that our soon-to-be-graduate of a Philadelphia institution arranges a spring break trip during which he will visit an automobile company in Detroit on a Monday, a Chicago bank on Tuesday, and a brewer in St. Louis on Wednesday. Sounds as if we have a problem. Not really. Our candidate could take an afternoon flight to Detroit Sunday so as to get a good night's sleep before his interview on Monday, fly to Chicago in the late afternoon on Monday, and go to St. Louis Tuesday evening. He could fly from St. Louis to Philadelphia the next night.

He calls his interviewer in Detroit and outlines his proposal. The two might conclude that an equitable arrangement would be for the three companies to split the air fare evenly and for each to pick up the tab for the hotel in its own city. Miscellaneous expenses could be allocated on the basis of where they were incurred. If this arrangement is agreeable to the interviewer in Detroit, our friend should call Chicago and St. Louis to secure their approval. If the applicant were really on the ball and as destitute as most of his classmates, he would have looked up plane schedules and ticket costs before he called Detroit. Had he done so, he could have offered to purchase the tickets and asked for an advance from each of the three companies to cover its share of the cost. For the auto company to buy the tickets, send them to Philadelphia, and collect from the bank and the brewer would be a needless complication. Each company could make the necessary hotel reservation.

It would be helpful if the applicant made copies of the tickets so that each company would have evidence of the expense for its files.

Companies do not frown on such programs; they heartily endorse them. The cost of such a program will be less than the cost of having the applicant make a visit to just one company, and there is nothing wrong in saving money. Companies realize that qualified applicants are in demand and will receive invitations from several potential employers. A multipurpose trip is also an advantage to the job hunter; it saves him time as well as wear and tear.

The one essential ingredient in all of this is that all parties know exactly what is happening.

An unscrupulous candidate who plans to visit three companies in Atlanta and cons each of them into paying for his transportation and lodging is nothing but a crook, and if he gets caught, as he probably will, he deserves whatever he gets. Honesty is the only policy, and don't you forget it.

Hints:

□ Level with everyone involved when you plan more than one visit on a trip.

☐ Make sure there is full understanding and agreement all around when you set up such a trip.

☐ Be aware that companies appreciate your efforts to save them money.

A couple of more suggestions, and then we'll wind up the subject of expenses. Suppose you have been invited to Jacksonville to visit an insurance company on a Friday. You have no classes until the following Thursday—lucky you. Your parents are spending the winter in their condominium in Palm Beach, and you would like to visit them for a couple of days and incidentally to soak up a bit of sun on the beach.

There is no reason why you shouldn't tell the insurance company what you would like to do and ask whether it will pay the cost of a round-trip ticket to Jacksonville. You would pay for the additional travel cost.

All right. Now, suppose you are flying from New Orleans to visit a consulting firm in Washington. You have a brother living there who is a lawyer with the Justice Department, and you will spend the night of your arrival at his apartment and then stay on for a day or two to see the sights.

Tell the consulting firm your plans. It will be pleased to save the exorbitant cost of a room at one of the better hotels. If it is sending you the airline tickets, it is entitled to know why you aren't returning to New Orleans directly after your visit. It would be distressed if it thought you planned to spend a day with another prospective employer at its expense.

I have been told that some applicants feel that in such an event, since the company is being saved the cost of a hotel room, it would not object if you entertained your brother for dinner at its expense. I don't agree. Your own dinner the night you arrive is a proper expense, but any entertainment you do is a personal expense, even though on balance you are saving money for the firm you are visiting. In addition, the company should not be charged for any local expenses that you incur after your interview if you could have been expected to have left for home before the expenses were incurred.

Expense accounts are a very tricky thing—ask any businessman who travels on his job. Be straightforward; be honest; be reasonable.

Hints:

□ Work out everything before you start a multipurpose trip. No loose ends.

□ Remember that a company will draw conclusions about your character from how you handle your expenses.

The final word on expenses. Suppose that after a campus interview a company invites you to visit its office 500 miles away. You are told that the company policy is not to pay expenses. What do you do? Simple. You've got to decide whether the probability of a job offer and the desirability of the job are worth the cost. A factor in your decision might be the company's refusal to assume an expense that most corporations view as one of the normal costs of recruiting employees. Fortunately, few of the major companies that interview on campus have adopted this policy.

On the other hand, if you secure an invitation to a corporate headquarters as the result of a direct mail campaign, it is not unusual for the company to expect you to make the visit at your own expense. I can see the justification for this attitude.

Postvisit actions

What do you do as soon as you return home from a visit? You should already know, but I'll refresh your memory.

1. Write your thank-you note. It is not necessary to send individual notes to everyone you met. The person who invited you is your prime target, and you might also want to refresh the memory of the individual who would be your big boss if he decides that an offer should be made to you. Don't forget the stroke to the company, a restatement of your interest, and a mention of the date by which you hope to hear from the company.

2. Enclose your expense account along with any receipts you might have collected. Be sure you have filled out the form accurately, and don't forget to sign it.

6

The résumé

Résumé, a noun lifted from the French language, means a summary, a short account of one's career and one's qualifications for a job. The word is pronounced either *raze-you-may* or *raze-zoo-may* because of the acute accent (´) over both *e*'s.

Resume is a verb with a number of meanings, among which are: begin again after an interruption, take again, reoccupy.

There are a few purists left in the world who are offended when they are confronted with the misuse of a word. One of them might even be the person you hope will offer you a job. Improve your chances by giving him a *résumé,* not a *resume*—whatever that might be. Never forget the accents when you write the word, and pronounce it correctly when you use it in speech.

What purpose does a résumé fill? It is an advertisement, a door opener. No matter how good your résumé is, there is only one chance in a thousand that it alone will get you a job, but a well-written résumé will keep you in the game, prevent your elimination from the next round of the job hunt. It is a necessary tool in all the many methods used to find the right job.

Some companies require a placement office to submit copies of résumés well in advance of a campus visit and interview an applicant only if his résumé leads them to believe that the individual might fit one of the job opportunities they have to offer.

Interviewers for other companies are not quite so discriminating and will pick up at the placement office the résumés submitted by students who have signed for an interview. Usually, such interviewers will find time to review these résumés and make preliminary judgments even before the applicant appears for his interview. Give yourself a break; get a good start by having an attractive, well-prepared résumé.

If you respond to an ad in *The Wall Street Journal* or your local newspaper, you will be asked to submit a résumé. It had better be a good one. The advertiser may receive hundreds of replies, and only a small percentage of them will deserve more than a casual glance.

If you engage in a letter writing campaign directed at a number of potential employers, the quality of your résumé as well as the content of your cover letter will determine the response you receive.

To an employment agency or a headhunter your résumé is the major selling point that will secure you an interview with the client.

Hints:

□ A good résumé won't get you a job, but a poor one can cost you the opportunity to even be considered for one.

□ Prepare your résumé carefully. Remember that couplet in Gray's *Elegy:* "Full many a flower is born to blush unseen/ And waste its sweetness on the desert air." Make sure your qualities are seen and appreciated where they will do you the most good.

What information should be included in a résumé?

Name, address, phone number

No comment necessary except don't forget your area code.

Job objective

This is where your earlier self-analysis will start to pay dividends. Specificity on this subject is essential. Recruiters— and who can blame them?—are not interested in an individual who states his objective in vague, general terms. If the applicant says he is looking for a job with a large corporation in the consumer product field, they want to know whether he is seeking a selling job or a staff assignment in the financial or planning department. Is the candidate interested in foods, drugs, or recreational equipment? The recruiter has specific openings to fill, and his first act is to match an opening with the objectives and qualifications shown in the résumés submitted to him.

An awkward complication results. If the résumé writer is too general, he will miss the boat with everyone; if he is too specific, he takes the chance of being bypassed by corporations and jobs slightly outside his stated target area.

One solution to this problem would be to prepare a hand-tailored résumé for each job opportunity that comes up. Such a procedure would not be feasible for most candidates. A practical solution is to be explicit in the job objective and not to specify too closely the preferred industry or company.

Here are some examples of this approach:

1. Position on corporate financial staff offering exposure to other functional areas in preparation for eventual general management responsibilities.
2. Line management position in a technology-oriented company.

3. Sales or line marketing position.
4. Financial management.
5. Position in advertising or line marketing management.
6. Position in corporate or municipal finance.
7. Position in marketing or product management involving either a domestic or multinational focus.
8. Position in corporate finance, planning, or investment management.
9. Position utilizing background in accounting, finance, and systems analysis in the area of management consulting, corporate finance, or planning.
10. Position in the area of general financial management and planning in a small corporation.

In the examples listed, you will note that only the second and the last refer to the type of company that interests the applicant. The second specifies a technology-oriented company, and the last specifies a small company. All the other objectives, to a greater or lesser extent, specify the type of work desired rather than the type of employer.

Thus, if an applicant desires a position in financial management, he does not restrict himself to companies in any particular industry. He would as soon work for General Electric as for General Foods so long as he stayed in his chosen field. At the same time he will be selective in the companies he interviews as he may have already decided that he would not be interested in working for a hotel chain or a public utility even if jobs in those areas were available.

Another approach to objectives is to concentrate on the type of company that interests you rather than the function you would like to perform in the company. Some examples of this approach follow.

1. Division-level management position in the life insurance industry.

2. Position in strategic planning with an industrial products company.
3. Position in investment banking or a venture capital organization.
4. Position in investment banking or investment management.
5. Position in marketing in a manufacturing organization.
6. Position in financial management with a consulting firm.

You will observe that all of these examples specify the type of company desired. You will also note that two of them fail to mention the type of job sought and that the first example listed is not even very enlightening as to the job wanted. Division-level management covers a lot of territory. Does the applicant desire a sales management job, does he wish to work on division budgets, or is his goal to be the office manager?

The individual who specifies a single industry deliberately rules out interest on the part of firms in any other line of endeavor. He places serious constraints on his options. Furthermore, if he does not indicate what type of work he is seeking in his chosen field, he risks being passed over by a recruiting firm which is hiring for a specific function.

It seems to me that a college senior with little previous experience would be making a serious mistake if he framed his job objective in such a restrictive manner. On the other hand, a master's candidate who spent four years with an investment bank before returning to school might not find such a statement of job objective to be a handicap. A later section of his résumé would list his banking experience and accomplishments.

Here is a third type of expression of objective:

A position in investment banking, commercial banking, or advertising.

What might be the reaction of a recruiter when he reads that statement? Advertising would appear to have little or nothing in common with either type of banking, and who could blame the recruiter if he paid slight attention to the rest of the résumé?

My advice to the author of this objective would be to prepare two separate résumés. One would stress his qualifications for banking work, and the other would highlight the creative aspects of his personality and experience. Furthermore, I would suggest that he spend more time in self-analysis in an attempt to determine more accurately what type of work he actually wanted.

A question might arise as to the applicant's longer term objectives. For relatively inexperienced applicants the primary focus is on securing an entry-level opportunity. Such an applicant is incompetent to plot a course for himself over the next 10 or 20 years. The more experience an individual has, the farther ahead his objectives should extend. In contrast to the college senior, a 35-year-old executive with an MBA who is contemplating a change of scenery should know where he wants to be at the end of this decade and even the next.

A college senior might express his objective this way:

> An entry-level position in consumer products marketing leading to a line position in management.

If I were a recruiter, I would like that statement. The applicant knows what he wants now, and at the same time he has aspirations for the future.

An MBA candidate might phrase his objective this way:

> Project evaluation and financial analysis in either a line or staff position with the ultimate objective of becoming director of research and planning.

A word of warning. Don't go too far in this direction. Consider an objective that states: "Position in marketing with opportunity to become vice president in eight years and company president by age 50." Few department heads would knowingly hire an assistant who has announced his intention to trample underfoot anyone obstructing his mad rush to the top. Take it easy; there are other, more acceptable ways to show your motivation and desire to succeed.

Hints:

☐ Don't unnecessarily narrow your objectives.

☐ Don't try to be all things to all people.

☐ Don't allow your stated objectives to be inconsistent.

☐ Don't go into minute detail on your plans for the rest of your life.

☐ Keep your stated objectives short.

In this section I appear to have said that if you are too general in your approach to objectives, you lose out because a recruiter might feel that you are uncertain of what you are looking for, while if you are too specific, you severely restrict the number of organizations which might be interested in you. Excellent. I agree with myself on those points. Now for the solution of the dilemma.

I recommend that in preparing your résumé, you reserve specificity for the definition of the type of work sought: sales, marketing, planning, research, finance, accounting, and so forth. Add a word or two about your plans for the future only if you feel qualified to do so. Do not be specific in your treatment of the type of organization or the industry that interests you. Remember, the résumé is only a door opener. During the interview you can demonstrate your interest in

and qualification for the opening under discussion. After all,
if you seek a financial planning job, R. J. Reynolds, General
Motors, or IBM could supply suitable opportunities. In short,
keep as many options open as you can. Let the résumé show
what type of work you are looking for—be positive about
that—and rely on your oral ability to show a recruiter that
your talents can be of value to his employer.

That approach makes sense to me. I hope it satisfies you.
One more suggestion. Be aware of the importance of this
section in your résumé even though it is only two or three
lines in length. Get your mind straight on your objectives—
relate them to each of your opportunities.

Education

The first thing to remember is to start with the present
and work backward. If you are now in graduate school, list
that first, then your college. In such a case, in the interest of
saving space it would not be necessary to give details of your
high school years. An exception to this suggestion would be
made if there was something unusual about your secondary
school education. If you spent two years in Zurich where you
became fluent in French and German, you should mention
that.

If you are a college senior and you enjoyed an outstanding
career in high school, you should mention your high school
achievements.

Be sure to highlight your major in college, especially if it
supports your qualifications for your job objective. However,
if you majored in philosophy, you should mention that fact
even though you suspect that it will not be of much help to
you in the eyes of a recruiter looking for an analyst for his
company's treasury department. If you had several courses

in accounting and economics, be sure to mention them, for he will be interested in that.

It is not essential that grade averages be stated in a résumé. Especially if you do not feel that they will do you credit. On the other hand, if you were a Phi Beta Kappa with a 3.96 average, you will understandably make that known.

At this point we'll digress for a few minutes on the subject of disclosing college and graduate school grades.

Grades are the principal determinant of whether or not you receive your diploma. In an academic environment they are of paramount importance. They are not nearly as important when you are being considered for a job. Don't misunderstand me; all other things being equal, the applicant with the highest grade average will probably be picked for a job opening. The fact is, however, that all other things are never equal. Grades are a factor—make no mistake about that—but in many instances they are outweighed by other considerations such as evidence of leadership qualities, motivation, personality, articulateness, extracurricular accomplishments—to name a few.

Thus, if you are proud of your grades, mention them. If you are a Phi Beta Kappa, say so. List the academic honors you have earned. Don't reveal less than excellent grades. Your academic record may or may not be requested by a potential employer. Let sleeping dogs lie until you are forced to wake them.

Many institutions, particularly graduate schools, do not disclose or even determine the class rankings of students, nor do they compute grade point averages. Their approach to this issue is that any student receiving a degree has met academic standards and that that should satisfy an employer.

A majority of corporations respect and accept this attitude, but some are mean enough to require a transcript of an applicant's record. Such a transcript will not be released until its release has been authorized by the student, and it is up to him to decide whether or not to make this information available. He must recognize the fact that he probably will not be considered for a job unless he accedes to the company's request.

The whole issue is a sticky one. I suppose you can't blame an employer if he wants to know what degree of smarts an applicant possesses. On the other hand, mitigating circumstances do account for poor grades in some instances, and students do mend their ways as their education progresses. If college grades were of paramount importance, many outstanding master's candidates would never have been admitted to graduate school and hosts of corporate presidents would still be looking for their first job.

It's a Catch 22 problem. If you disclose your grades and they are poor, you won't get the job. If you keep them a secret, you won't either. You pay your money and take your choice.

Of course, the best remedy is to have made good grades—you probably could have if you had put your mind to it. The problem arose because there were other important demands on your time and efforts at the moment. It could be that those activities were of even greater importance than whether you received a B+ or a B in a course. In such a case, play up your accomplishments. After all, what is the basic purpose of an education?

Hints:

□ If you are proud of your grades, blow your horn loud and clear.

□ If you aren't, keep a low profile and hope that you are not closely questioned on them.

□ If you are required to submit a transcript, let your conscience be your guide and be prepared to accept the result of refusing to do so.

□ If you do submit a transcript of poor grades and there are mitigating circumstances—nonchronic illness, the need to work your way through school—make sure the causes are known.

□ In all cases, build your application on your strengths—don't let your weaknesses dynamite you.

□ Don't start worrying about your grades three months before you expect to graduate. The sooner you realize that your grades may have an influence on your ability to get the job you want, the more you can do to bring them up to respectable levels.

Having disposed of that digression, let's get back to the education section of your résumé. In addition to the statistics of your schooling, you should enumerate your curricular and extracurricular achievements. If you were a class officer, say so. Likewise for memberships and offices in social organizations. Athletic activity can be mentioned even though it was on intramural levels.

We'll look at a few examples of this part of a résumé, starting with one written by a college senior.

EDUCATION   Pulaski College—candidate for BA, June 19XX. Major in European history with minor in economics. Electives included courses in accounting, business law, and finance. Grade average 3.5 of possible 4.0. Dean's list senior year. Treasurer of _____ fraternity; assistant editor of college newspaper; member of History Club and Business Association. Varsity soccer three years; intramural basketball and tennis.

Pleasant Valley High School—graduated 19XX. Class president junior and senior years; varsity soccer and basketball. Ranked fourth in class of 163.

Now for a bit of analysis. Our friend wisely did not go into the subject matter of his senior thesis, which happened to concern itself with Monmouth's ill-fated attempt to usurp the throne of Britain in 1685. He was interested in the subject and learned much from his research, but a possible employer would be more impressed by the economics and business courses he took.

His grades in school and college were extremely good, so he mentioned them. His extracurricular experiences were varied and rather impressive. He had held positions of responsibility, and the fact that he was elected class officer in school and held offices in college indicate that he was liked and respected by his peers. A good job.

Here's another example.

EDUCATION Pulaski College—candidate for BA, June 19XX. Varsity football four years, captain senior year; varsity basketball three years. _____ fraternity; president Y society (social club). Major in sociology. Grade point average 2.3.

Pleasant Valley High School—graduated 19XX. Nine letters in three sports. State championship team in baseball.

If you were a recruiter, what impression would you have after reading this excerpt from a résumé? Could you be blamed if you concluded that the individual was an unreconstructed jock whose main interests were fun and games? You might also wonder why he disclosed his less than impressive grade average, and you might evince surprise that in the last seven years he had accomplished nothing that he considered worthy of mention besides sports and membership in a drinking society. Even if the recruiter was searching for a high school football coach, he would look for as well rounded a candidate as he could find.

A master's candidate in business administration might frame his answer this way:

EDUCATION The Palmolive School of Business Administration, candidate for MBA, June 19XX. Finance Club (Treasurer), Entrepreneurs Club, Honor Committee, Washington Award recipient.

Pulaski College—BS biology, 19XX. Graduated summa cum laude. Student Council, Debating Society, varsity crew, and rugby.

Such a statement covers a lot of ground in a few words. You will note that the author did not employ normal sentence structure. There are few verbs and no pronouns. He did not write, "I did this or that." He kept it short. Good for him. Consider how the same material might have been stated.

EDUCATION I am a candidate for an MBA degree from the Palmolive School of Business Administration in June of 19XX. I am a member and Treasurer of the Finance Club, a member of the Entrepreneurs Club and the Honor Committee. I received the Washington Award.

I graduated from Pulaski College in 19XX with a BS in biology. I graduated summa cum laude. I was a member of the Student Council and the Debating Society, and I was on the varsity crew and the rugby team.

Prolix—slow reading. A résumé should be not long-winded but succinct. Personal pronouns should be avoided.

Note also that neither résumé itemized the courses taken in graduate school. Palmolive is in the top rank of business schools, and its graduates are generalists rather than specialists. Qualified recruiters know this and understand that all its students are well grounded in the basics of management theory and practice.

If the student is attending a graduate school where majors and minors are elected, as in college, he would indicate his course of study in this section.

Hints:

☐ Make it short and sweet. Eliminate personal pronouns.

☐ Indicate, if possible, that you are a mature, well-rounded person.

☐ Refer to your strengths—reinforce them. Don't draw attention to weaknesses such as poor grades.

Work experience

Again we're going to differentiate between the college and the graduate school student. It is quite probable that a college senior's experiences will have been confined to summer jobs with perhaps part time employment during the school year to help pay expenses, while a graduate student may have spent several years working before returning to school.

No college senior should be ashamed of his lack of formal full time work experience and it will not be held against him by a recruiter. What he is looking for in an applicant are evidences of motivation, successes in enterprises undertaken, wise utilization of available time. Paramount in his mind is whether the applicant has profited from whatever experience he may have had.

Work experience should be listed in chronological order beginning with the present and continuing backward.

Ann Marshall, a college senior, will graduate this spring. This is what she writes.

EXPERIENCE   **19XX Summer.**
Intern with E. I. Du Pont, Wilmington, Delaware. Accounting Department—worked on accounts receivable and collection of delinquent accounts.

19XX Summer.
Counselor at camp for underprivileged children.

19XX Summer.

Salesperson—dress shop.

Worked way through college as mathematics tutor, waitress, lab assistant.

A few comments on this transcript. The dress shop is not identified. What recruiter could be expected to have heard of La Boutique in Selma, Alabama? Du Pont is referred to by name. It is familiar to everyone, and Ann probably would not have secured even a summer job with it if she had not had something special to offer. Her work at Du Pont is described.

Ann did not name the summer camp. If a recruiter were interested in her work there, he could question her during the interview. Taking this type of position indicates that Ann has a sense of social obligation and probably enjoys being with children.

An employer would be impressed by Ann's industry during her college years. Anyone who works her way through college earns high marks for motivation. Tutoring in math shows that she must be competent in the field, and being a waitress indicates that she considered no job beneath her dignity. There is nothing wrong with any honest labor, and being a waitress assures a person of at least one good meal a day.

All in all, a recruiter would be impressed by Ann's experience, unprepossessing as it may appear to be on the surface.

Hints:

□ Properly expressed, almost every experience can cast a favorable light on your personality and character.

□ You don't have to beat the drum or clash the cymbals to get your point across.

What if your economic circumstances were the opposite of Ann's and you neither had summer jobs nor found it necessary to provide any part of your college expenses? Instead of

122

working, you spent summers backpacking in the Rockies, making the grand tour of Europe, and playing the amateur golf or tennis circuit. So what? Who says it's a crime to enjoy life? You'll probably spend the next 40 years working like the rest of us. The family allowance will cease when you graduate, and getting the groceries on the table will become an economic necessity.

Should such a happy situation have been your lot, simply ignore the experience section of your résumé. Be prepared, however, for questions on how you spent your summers. Travel is a broadening experience; the circuit should have taught you how to handle yourself and meet people; and backpacking not only keeps you in shape but makes you self-reliant.

A recruiter will, of course, be aware of your lack of work experience, but extracurricular activities in school and college and well-developed outside interests should fill the void without damage to your prospects.

Hints:

☐ If you have no job experience, don't apologize for lacking it.
☐ Build on other aspects of your character and personality that will replace the missing factor.

So far, so good. Now comes the master's candidate. His experience should be wider than the college senior's: he has two more summers to account for, and he may have worked full time for one or more years. In such an event, for the purpose of saving space, he will shorten the coverage of his college days and concentrate on his more recent doings.

EXPERIENCE **19XX Summer.**
Arkansas Limestone Corp., Little Rock. Developed marketing strategy for limestone aggregate company.

19XX July to 19XX September (a little over two years)
Jefferson National Bank, Baltimore, Md. Started in credit department, promoted to Assistant Vice President shortly before resignation. Handled a portfolio of active corporate accounts. Responsible for financial analysis, credit decisions, and cross-selling of services. One half of time spent in development of new business.

Summer and part-time work during college included selling encyclopedias, managing student food services, working in California vineyards.

You will note that this gentleman explained his duties on his most recent summer job and on the full-time banking position he held. Recruiters are interested in the kinds of work you have done. This student gave less detail on his earlier experiences at a lower level but described the types of work that he did.

One more example from a graduate school student, and then we'll wind up this section.

EXPERIENCE   **19XX—Summer**
General Electric Company. Prepared analyses for appliance products group and recommended course of action.

19XX July to 19XX August (three years)
Jackson International Publishing Company. Sold advertising space in seven international business magazines. Increased division business 150 percent by adding new clients such as United Airlines, American Express and Manufacturers Hanover Trust.

Summer work prior to 19XX included internship with Arthur Andersen, Research and Development Division of Western Electric, and Purchasing Department of Union Carbide.

Succinct, yet we get an excellent picture of this individual. Note how he lists his responsibilities on each job. Note also that where he distinguished himself by increasing sales markedly, he does not hesitate to make the fact known. Another thing—he is a great name-dropper. If you get summer jobs with the cream of the crop, why not let it be known? It proves you had what it took to impress the very best.

Hints:

- Tighten your writing as much as possible.
- Stay away from personal pronouns. No *I*'s or *my*'s.
- Complete sentences are desirable but not essential. Smoothness is needed, however.
- Blow your horn if you have the opportunity. Brag a little about your accomplishments if they exist. Don't make them up.
- If you have the ammunition, name-drop to improve your image.
- Hit the high spots. The most recent experience is the most important.

A final, final word before we close. None of the excerpts we have quoted mention salary on either summer of full-time jobs. I recommend a policy of omitting references to pay from résumés. If you have full-time experience, list promotions and added responsibilities assumed, but don't say what you got paid. A résumé is not the place to divulge past earnings or future salary expectations.

There is always an exception to any precept. If you had a truly incredible experience on a summer job, it should be mentioned. I know one young lady, a born salesperson, who took a selling job with a nursery for eight weeks one summer and made an astonishing $15,000 during that period. She mentioned this in her résumé—and rightly so—not as an indication that she expected to start a regular job in a sales capacity at $100,000 a year, but as proof of her exceptional ability.

Personal remarks

This is a catchall section which will contain any information you feel is important enough to include in your résumé and can't find anywhere else to put it.

For a change of pace we'll start with examples, comment on them, and make suggestions as we go along.

PERSONAL Date of birth: August 23, 19XX. Weight: 160 pounds. Height: 6'00". Health: excellent. Marital status: single. I enjoy racket games, swimming, and travel.

The information contained here is scarcely earth shattering. To use a word that disgusts me every time I see it, the personal revelation is not every "insightful." The résumé states our friend's college graduation year, and it isn't important to me whether his birthday is August 23 or July 10. He is single—fine. Height and weight are important to an interviewer mainly if they indicate abnormality of size or shape. If a résumé contains a picture, exact statistics are unnecessary.

The fact that the gentleman enjoys swimming, racket sports, and travel fails to differentiate him from 99 percent of his classmates.

On top of all this, I don't care for the writing style. All those capital letters and proliferation of punctuation marks make for slow, jerky reading.

Nothing personal comes through. The individual does little to attract me to him. He isn't selling himself.

This one is still worse.

PERSONAL   I am a white Roman Catholic, and I have always been opposed to oppression of all people less fortunate than me. I am a strong supporter of the ERA and a member of the ACLU. I am active in community affairs and a member of numerous civic groups.

Don't get me wrong: I have no religious or racial prejudices. It is the right of every individual to have strong feelings on women's rights and civil liberties. That is just fine by me, but—and it's a big but—is this the place to mount your charger and expound your philosophy to the world? I think not. What would be the probable reaction of the recruiter when he read that passage?

In addition, I don't approve the constant use of the personal pronoun or the incorrect case of one of them.

Here's another.

PERSONAL   Married, no children. Read and speak Spanish and Portuguese. Interested in politics, sports, travel, and reading.

And still another:

PERSONAL   Born in Syracuse, New York. Father in diplomatic service. Lived several years in Frankfurt, Rome, London. Fluent in German and Italian. Interests include classical music, singing, WW II history, theater, and visual arts.

The flavor of the writer is beginning to come through. I get a feel for that young woman's personality and talents.

The final example:

PERSONAL   Age 30. Married—son 6, daughter 4. Create and sell Calder-type mobiles. Licensed pilot and aircraft mechanic. Build and fly hang gliders. Scoutmaster and YMCA youth counselor. Remodel houses—masonry, plumbing, carpentry.

An unusual man—I'll agree that not all of us are equally gifted, but when I read those few lines, I have a pretty good idea what kind of person wrote them. He is, of course, an engineer, and I'll wager that a number of manufacturers will want to hire him. I would.

Hints:

□ Avoid the use of personal pronouns.

□ Don't make this section a chronicle of vital statistics.

□ Disclose interesting facets of your personality.

□ Focus on areas that distinguish you from others:
   1. Living abroad—foreign languages.
   2. Unusual or profitable hobbies.
   3. Involvement in civic or charitable affairs.

□ Don't philosophize or preach on your standards of behavior or your social beliefs.

□ Remember that this is about the only opportunity a résumé gives you to sell your personality and differentiate yourself from many of your classmates with similar backgrounds.

References

There are two schools of thought on this subject. One holds that references should be included in the résumé, and, quite logically, the other maintains that they should not. I prefer to see no names listed and either no mention made of the subject or, if you wish a notation like this:

REFERENCES Will be furnished on request.

There are several reasons why I take this attitude. It is unlikely that a recruiter would check references before the first interview with an applicant. Why, then, clutter the résumé with unnecessary information? If a student interviews a number of potential employers and several of them as a matter of policy write to each of the individuals listed as references, these family friends and long-suffering faculty members will scarcely be overjoyed at the prospect of replying to each of the potential employers individually.

There is plenty of time to hand out a list of references. Wait until they are specifically requested or until negotiations have proceeded to the point that employment is a real probability rather than a remote possibility.

Yet, always be ready with a list of four or so individuals who can be counted on to report favorably on you. Even a screening interview can be so successful that an applicant may be asked for references.

You should secure permission from every individual you hope to use as a reference, and you should gain approval before you submit a name to a prospective employer.

What type of person should you seek as a reference? A couple of faculty members make a good start. Pick only ones with whom you have established a personal relationship. The fact that Professor Higgins gave you A's in both the courses you took under him would not make him a good reference if your only contact with him consisted of a nod when you attended his lectures or an occasional "Good morning" when you encountered him in the corridor.

Family friends are good sources of references, particularly if they have achieved a position of eminence in your community. The words of a bank president carry more weight than a letter from a neighbor whose lawn you used to cut five years ago.

Don't use relatives as references. They may endow you with all the finest characteristics of Sir Galahad, Superman and Abraham Lincoln, but the fact that the glowing report was written by Uncle Elmer might render it suspect by the reader.

Former employers are excellent references, provided they

can be counted on to give you a favorable send-off. In other words, be careful in choosing the people to whom you entrust your chances for a job.

Should you be fortunate enough to be a member of a family intimate with senators, Supreme Court justices, and Rockefellers and Du Ponts, use only one or two of such illustrious individuals as references. Beware of overkill, and think of the reaction of the recruiter trying to fill a line job in a heavy manufacturing plant. Will you be too good for the job?

Choose your references from as wide a spectrum as possible: one or two teachers who think well of both your personality and your academic ability, a family friend who has known you since childhood, a community leader, a former employer who has a high regard for your skills and your ability to get along with fellow workers.

I don't particularly care for "To whom it may concern" letters of recommendation. There is something cold about them that turns me off. What usually happens is that a job hunter gets a prominent person—for instance, a bank president friend of his father—to write an excellent letter. He gets the letter reproduced and attaches a copy to every résumé he submits. A letter of recommendation should be warm, personal, not a canned replay.

Here's another reason for not listing references in a résumé. Suppose that you are looking for a job as a security analyst in either a commercial or an investment bank, and suppose further that you can use as references a senior vice president of the Chemical Bank and a partner in Salomon Brothers. You would give one name to the commercial bank and the other name to the investment bank. Your reference may be known, at least by reputation, by the recruiter. If he is, so much the better for you.

Line up as many references as you can, with as broad coverage as possible of the industries you are interested in. Then, pick from your list the individuals who are closest to the area in which you are seeking a job.

In most cases, if a person consents to act as a reference for you, he is flattered that you have chosen him and will do his best to write a favorable but honest report on you. Out of courtesy to him, don't force him to write letter after letter extolling your virtues to companies you don't really want to work for. Be selective, and be considerate of the people who have offered to help you.

Hints:

□ Don't list names of references on your résumé.

□ Either say nothing about references, or state: "References will be furnished on request."

□ Always ask permission before submitting the name of a reference.

□ Don't tax the time or patience of an individual by overuse of his name.

□ Try for a wide selection of individuals: bankers, lawyers, merchants, manufacturers, teachers, and so forth.

□ Select references related to the field in which you are applying.

□ Use only faculty members with whom you have established a personal relationship.

□ Beware of overkill. Don't swamp a small manufacturing plant in Arkansas with a deluge of fulsome letters from national political figures or industrial giants.

Preparation of a résumé

So much for what goes into a résumé. Now, let's talk about what it should look like.

For an overwhelming majority of soon-to-be-graduated students a one-page résumé is sufficient. A standard 8½-by-11-inch sheet is recommended, and the paper should be of good quality. Don't painstakingly type out a poorly spaced résumé, replete with erasures and misspellings, and then make 60 duplicates on a copying machine. A professional printing job is much more desirable, and even if it costs you a few dollars, don't forget—your résumé might open the door for you to join a company that could pay you several million over the next 40 years. Setting type for a single-page résumé will cost in the neighborhood of $12-15, and printing 60 copies will add no more than $5. Money well spent.

Another advantage of using a professionally printed résumé is that this enables you to reproduce your picture. The picture should be placed in the upper right-hand corner of the résumé. It need be only 1½ inches wide and 2 inches high, and it should show the head and the upper torso. Men should be wearing coat and tie when they sit for their picture. Nether extremities may be clad in blue jeans, and feet may be bare—they won't show—but be sure that what does show is properly clad and groomed. Women should dress like businesswomen, not like prom queens posing for a publicity shot. No plunging necklines, diamond tiaras, or dangling earrings—except if you are applying for a job in a Las Vegas floor show, in which case you should supply several 8-by-10 glossy full-length photos.

Double-space between sections, and give each section a title. Allow ample margin all the way around. White space is essential; don't fill the page with writing. Nothing turns a reader off faster than being presented with a solid mass of black ink.

Make a rough draft of your résumé. Is it too long to fit on a single page? If so, you probably have not written concisely. If it is too short, you have not supplied enough information about yourself. In either case you should revise and rewrite.

How about your spelling and grammar? Have you eliminated personal pronouns? Ask a couple of friends or even a member of your faculty to edit and comment. If the placement department of your school is willing, ask a member for advice. Listen to what everyone says. If the advice you receive makes sense, follow it, but don't allow another person to prepare your résumé for you. It is a personal document, and it should have the coloring of your own personality. Résumés prepared by professionals lack this necessary ingredient.

Check the organization of material. Does the finished product please the eye?

It is unnecessary and undesirable to date a résumé. You will be using copies of the résumé over a period of several months, and the résumé shouldn't indicate how long ago it was written.

When you have edited, revised, corrected, and rearranged ad infinitum, and the résumé finally meets with your approval, have it typed by an expert. Check again for typos, and submit the finished product along with a picture to the printer. By this time you will be heartily sick of the whole deal. Your spirits will revive when you pick up the stack of beautifully printed sheets that will be a joy to behold and will read as if they were written by a budding Homer.

Now for a couple of sample résumés. The first is for a college senior, and the second was prepared by a candidate for a master's degree in business administration.

Gimmicks

"Stay away from them" is good advice. Don't use fancy colored paper with attractively designed borders. Don't go for unusual organization, no matter how artistic or eye-

LAURA ANN MONROE
116 Heights Road
Charlottesville, Virginia 22901
Telephone: (804) 294-6114

EMPLOYMENT OBJECTIVE	Position in product management with consumer products company in food or cosmetic field.
EDUCATION	**September 19XX to present** Candidate for BS degree in home economics, University of Virginia, Charlottesville, Virginia. Course emphasis in management of food services. President, Alpha Chi Sorority; Home Economics Council; dean's list four years; intramural basketball and field hockey.
	At high school in Leverett, West Virginia, class officer junior and senior year; editor of school paper.
EXPERIENCE	**May-August 19XX** Ramada Inn, Hyattsville, Maryland, Food Services Department. Assisted purchasing agent; revised menus; prepared cost studies on kitchen expenses.
	May-August 19XX Miller & Rhoads (department store), Richmond, Virginia. Demonstrated cosmetic products; trained and supervised other demonstrators in four stores.
	Worked part time during college and high school as a waitress and retail saleswoman in specialty shops.
PERSONAL	Single. Health excellent. Will locate anywhere in continental United States. Enjoy tennis and swimming; hobbies include photography, reading, history, and playing ragtime music on the piano.
REFERENCES	Will be supplied on request.

THOMAS P. McMULLEN
21-68 Copeley Hill
Charlottesville, Virginia 22903
Telephone: (804) 298-3030

EMPLOYMENT OBJECTIVE	Position in operations planning or financial control, with emphasis on data processing and management information systems.
EDUCATION	**September 19XX to present** Colgate Darden Graduate School of Business Administration, University of Virginia, Charlottesville, Virginia. Candidate for MBA degree in May 19XX. Member Finance Club; section representative; received Shermet honorary award.
	September 19XX to May 19XX University of Pennsylvania, Philadelphia, Pennsylvania. BS in mathematics. Graduated with honors; member Student-Faculty Committee; tutored in math and statistics. Captain tennis team; Ivy League and Eastern Intercollegiate singles champion.
EXPERIENCE	**May-August 19XX** Pittsburgh National Bank. Operations research analyst. Analyzed, reported, and presented recommendations on branch automation and on management reporting system for the computer center.
	July 19XX to August 19XX (three years) Territory manager for Burroughs Corporation, Columbus, Ohio. Sold and installed in-house computer systems and on-line terminal systems. Made sales proposals at board meetings. Planned and ran seminars for customers. Surpassed sales quota each year.
	Summer and part-time work during school and college included programming jobs using a wide variety of computers.
PERSONAL	Single. Health excellent. Will locate anywhere in world. Father a career army man. Lived abroad six years. Fluent in French and German. Interested in foreign affairs, modern history, photography, and tennis.
REFERENCES	Will be supplied on request.

catching it might be. Stick with a good quality of white or just off-white paper. Adopt the standard format used in our examples. Don't improvise or let your fancy run away with you.

An argument might be made for a divergence from this policy if you are applying for a creative job with an advertising agency. In that case you might want to allow your talent to pervade your résumé. OK, if you must, but I'd rather see you project your genius during an interview rather than try to capture it in a résumé. Remember, your résumé is a door opener—don't let it close doors in your face.

Hints:

☐ Your first résumé draft will be terrible.

☐ Your second won't be much better.

☐ Revise, rewrite, edit—again and again.

☐ Proofread your final draft for grammar, spelling, punctuation, construction.

☐ Seek advice and help from your placement office.

☐ Ditto from a literate faculty member.

☐ Don't let anybody, anybody at all, prepare your résumé for you. It must be your work.

☐ Have a professional printer produce your résumé.

☐ Get his advice on the spacing and size of type.

☐ Specify 8½-by-11 white or barely off-white paper of good quality.

☐ Don't allow your résumé to be more than one page in length.

☐ Include a photo if possible.

☐ Avoid gimmicks.

☐ Stay with a standard format.

7

Offers and rejections

Handling offers

The great day arrives when you receive a letter in the mail from a company you interviewed a month ago and visited two weeks ago. It is a good company, one of your top choices, and even though you tell yourself it is just another rejection, your fingers are not quite steady as you open the envelope. You read:

Dear Hank:

I am delighted to make you an offer of employment in the Finance Department of our company. The position carries a base salary of $_____ and in addition will entitle you to the standard benefits we have discussed.

If you accept our offer, Mr. Thompson would like you to start work on August 1. We are naturally desirous of learning your decision in the near future.

Please call me collect as soon as you can.

Sincerely,

J. B. Williams

137

Hank is in no position to reach for the phone at that instant. He's got a lot of good hard thinking to do before he places the call. At the same time he can't delay too long. Mr. Williams has offered a valuable gift—an excessively tardy response might make him feel that the offer was not appreciated.

Postponing decision

Perhaps Hank has received another offer already and is awaiting responses from two other companies he has visited. He realizes that it would not be wise for him to make a definite commitment one way or the other until the word is in from all the organizations with which he is negotiating. He'll need at least three weeks more before he can be sure he knows exactly where he stands. Mr. Williams' company is top grade. The opening in the Finance Department is right up Hank's alley; the job involves heavy responsibilities and will give him decision-making authority. The salary mentioned is 5 percent higher than Hank's other offer, and the company benefits are at least as good. If Hank had only two offers to consider, he would accept the one just received, but he is still waiting for word from Exxon and General Electric. He owes it to himself not to make a final decision until he hears from them. Earlier in the week Hank had spent on hour at the placement office studying the statistics that had already been developed on offers made to others in his class. His offer is above average, but Hank feels it should be. After all, his experience should place a premium on his value.

Late that afternoon Hank calls Mr. Williams.

Hello, Mr. Williams. This is Hank Moore at Jefferson College. You asked me to call.

Good to talk to you, Hank. What's your reaction to our offer?

I'm flattered and very grateful. I certainly appreciate it.

Good. Have you made a decison?

I'd like to talk to you about that, Mr. Williams, and I'd like to lay my cards on the table. I have received an offer from another company. It's a good company and an excellent opportunity, but if I had to make a choice now, I'd come with you. Right now, the problem is that I'm waiting to hear from two other corporations, and I feel I owe it to myself to consider all my options before I make a choice. Can you give me three weeks to get back to you? It might even be sooner.

So far, so good. Hank has done the right thing in asking for time, and Mr. Williams has been around long enough to know that Hank's reaction is the normal one. He will probably accept Hank's time schedule. If he does, all is well. What can Hank say, however, if he is told that the company wants to fill its openings as quickly as possible and must receive an answer within three or four days?

All Hank can do is agree to make his decision by the appointed date and go into consultation with himself. He can call the companies he is waiting to hear from, state his problem, and ask what his chances are with them. They may or may not speed up their schedule; many of the most prestigious companies do not respond favorably to efforts to steamroller them.

A company's demand for an immediate answer leaves a bad taste in the mouth of the person who is offered the job. He or she doesn't like to be pressured into a premature decision on a matter that is so important. The majority of companies realize this and more often than not are concerned with the dilemma of the applicant. Personally, I am irritated by the arrogance of a company that says, in effect, "Here is an offer. Take it or leave it. Immediately." Would I enjoy working in such an environment?

It may be that this company is Hank's first choice. He may

consider his chances for further offers not good, and even if he received them, he would not consider them to be equal to the present one. Even so, Hank should ask for a few days—say a week—before making a commitment.

Thus, when Mr. Williams asks for his reaction, Hank might say, "The offer sounds great. I want to thank you. Can you give me a few days to think it over? It's a big decision for me, and I want to be sure I do the right thing. How soon do you need to know?"

Mr. Williams will probably say, "I understand your feelings, Hank. Give me a call by this time next week. I do hope you'll accept our offer. We really want you with us. In the meantime, if you have any questions, get in touch."

Hints:

- If you need time to arrive at a decision on an offer, do not hesitate to ask for it.
- Be reasonable in your request. Three weeks may not be too long; three months certainly is.
- Make the best use of the time that is given you.

Postponing starting date

In our previous example Hank was told that the company would like him to start work the first of August. That would give him almost two months to get organized and, incidentally, to take a few weeks off for a trip down the Colorado River with friends—a project he had been planning for years. What if he were asked to report for work on June 15?

Again, I would suggest that Hank be candid in his response. There is no reason why he shouldn't mention his plans. Perhaps it would make little difference to the company if he started July 15 instead of June 15. On the other hand, the company might have been planning a three-month indoctrination course for newly hired college graduates and may have wanted them to undertake it together. In such an event Hank would have to decide between the trip and the job.

Hint:

□ State your feelings, but don't act abrasively. Don't start giving yourself a reputation for being hard to get along with.

Moving expenses

Another matter that often arises is the question of moving expenses. As a general rule, companies do not pick up the tab for these expenses of college graduates, most of whom are single and whose worldly possessions, consisting of clothing, stereo equipment, and tennis rackets, will fit into the back seat of a VW. It is up to such new employees to make their own arrangements to report for work on the appointed day.

The situation is different for master's degree graduates. They are older; many of them are married; and they have accumulated enough furniture to fill a small apartment. In addition, they will begin work at a higher level than college graduates. For such new employees, a number of companies, as a matter of policy, expect to pay moving expenses and even travel costs to the job location. Some do not.

Hints:

□ Ask for company policy on moving expenses during an office visit.
□ If the opportunity does not arise at an earlier time, ask when you receive an offer.
□ Don't let this go until you have moved and have no idea what to do with the bill.

Choosing among offers

Now, let's get back to the problem of making a choice among several options. Suppose Hank receives offers from the other two companies and then has a week left to make up his mind which offer to accept. This is, without doubt, the most difficult part of the entire job seeking process. If an applicant has only one offer, his choice is simple. He either accepts, or he prepares for gradual starvation. When he has a variety of opportunities, he should base his decision on a careful analysis of the factors involved.

Filling in a chart might be helpful. Here is an example in which 1 represents top desirability and 3 the lowest ranking.

	Company A	Company B	Company C
Industry	1	1	3
Company	1	3	2
Location	3	3	2
Job	2	3	1
Prospects	1	2	2
People	2	1	3
Benefits	2	3	1
Salary	2	1	3
Total	14	17	17

Other criteria might be added based on the personal values of the applicant. Grading offers is not an easy job. One must attempt to be objective when assessing the relative qualities of the various offers. In this connection, beware of a simple arithmetic solution. In the above example company A is the winner on a mathematical basis, but are all the criteria of equal value? A chart can be helpful, but it is only a guide.

Prospects for the industry and the standing of the particular company in its field are certainly important elements in the decision-making process. Some industries do have better prospects than others, and one company may have better management, better products, and a more adequate capital structure than another.

Perhaps you have set your heart on getting a job in Boston and none of the companies that have made you an offer have offices within a thousand miles of the Athens of America. You have a choice among Chicago, Los Angeles, and New Orleans. None of these cities turns you on, but all of them have major sports teams and symphony orchestras. What about living conditions? How do rent and housing costs compare? Government departments publish cost-of-living charts for all the major cities in the country. Will your dollar go further in one place than another?

The job itself and the prospects it offers for further advancement are certainly of vital interest to you. The duties called for on one job may not be as interesting as the work you would do on another, but in the first case the opportunity for a transfer and increased responsibilities within two years may be much more probable. What is the value of this greater opportunity to you?

The quality of the people you will work with can make a dull job a worthwhile experience or a good job a bore. What was your impression of the company executives and lower management when you met them during an office visit? How would you define your relations with the company representatives during your discussions?

It might strike you as strange that on this chart benefits and salary have been left for last. They are important—make no mistake about that—but unless a company passes the first tests in adequate fashion, a wise applicant will never find it necessary to reach this point in his analysis. To exaggerate somewhat, who would take a high-paying job with a company about to file for bankruptcy?

The package of salary and benefits should be considered together. One company's salary offer may be a thousand dollars less than another's, yet its insurance and retirement plans may make the package far superior. Starting salary is important, but what you might be earning in five years is even more important. Don't forget that your future worth to a company depends to a large degree on the value of your contribution to it. Starting salary is only a base for your future potential. Yet, an applicant should expect any offer from a top-grade company to be competitive.

Hints:

☐ Analyze all offers carefully.

☐ Establish criteria for evaluating offers.

☐ Establish in your mind the relative values you place on these criteria.

☐ When your analysis is complete and indicates what choice should be made, ask yourself whether you would be happy with your decision. In short, are there intangibles that should also be considered?

Jobs—stepping stones or life sentences

Let us now digress for a moment or two on the subject of salary and entry-level jobs. Voluminous statistics have been compiled on the subject of the length of service to be expected on a job taken by a college or graduate school graduate. Many companies expect a 50 percent turnover within two years. In some industries and job classifications the rate is even higher. The point is that no graduate should base his job decision on the expectation that he will spend a lifetime with the company he elects to go with on his graduation.

Indeed, some graduates deliberately take the job that offers the most money with the intention of switching in a year or two. They feel that their prospects for a better position are enhanced by the greater salary they earn on the first job.

I am reminded of the experience of a friend of mine. We both graduated from college the same year, hitting the job market at its lowest ebb in human memory. His first job was in a retail store at $14 a week. Within a period of five years he held 16 jobs with 16 different employers, switching every time he found someone who would pay him a dollar or two more than he had been getting. He made one change for a 50-cent increase. All this happened in that remote past when, if you made $20 a week, you received $20 in your pay envelope every Friday. No tax withholding, no social security, no health insurance, no nothing except $20. My friend's theory was that switching brought him pay increases more rapidly than staying on one job and waiting for a raise. During this phase of his career he was a bill collector, a mortician, a carpenter, an insurance salesman, a punch press operator, a bank teller—you name it, he did it. Ultimately, he achieved one of the top jobs in the Federal Reserve System. On the other hand, I took a different route and remained with the same company until my retirement. Oddly enough, when we wound up our careers, Charley and I were as alike as two peas in a pod. There may be a message in this, but if there is, it escapes me.

My point is that no individual should necessarily plan to stay with the same employer for a lifetime. What he should do is take a job that is compatible with his interests and capabilities, work to his best ability, and then determine whether his efforts are being rewarded to his satisfaction. If so, he should remain where he is; if not, he should look for a change. An individual might even take a job to gain experience in an area he considers important to him with the intention of switching to another company as soon as he gains the missing ingredient. Companies are not unaware that job switching is widespread. They realize that it is a part of life and one of the penalties of having a preeminent reputation in a specialized area. How many salespeople of a well-known computer firm leave after a few years and take better positions with one of its competitors?

Another example. A young college graduate from the deep South took a job with a giant New York bank, intending to stay long enough to earn a title and then, with proven ability behind him, to return to the South and join an Atlanta bank. Not a bad plan at all. He was smart enough to realize that it was to his advantage to apply himself diligently while in New York. Fifteen years have passed, and he is still with the same bank. As he matured, so did his objectives. His advancement at the bank in assignments that interested him was so rapid that he realized he was better able to achieve his revised goals in New York.

As we grow older, our attitudes do change, and this is as it should be. No job should be considered a lifetime commitment, but every job should command the best efforts of the individual. It is shortsighted to give less than your best in any circumstance, and who knows what the future holds?

Keep your ear cocked for the first knock of opportunity at your door, but understand that opportunity can occur within your company as frequently as outside it.

Hints:

☐ Taking a job is not a life sentence.

☐ Employers expect a large turnover after two or three years of employment—some expect it even earlier.

☐ No onus is attached to job switching not caused by repeated failure to perform adequately.

□ On the other hand, there is little reason to switch jobs if you are happy and progressing to your satisfaction.

□ Realize that every job will be accompanied by problems. Compare the problems you have with those you might encounter on the job you are considering switching to.

Now, let's get back to what we were talking about, which was salary. What should you do if you are considering two offers that are almost equally desirable. The company you are leaning toward has offered a salary 10 percent lower than that offered by the other company. Both companies are grade A; both openings are in the same city, so no difference in cost of living is involved. You realize that you would not be making a mistake in accepting either job, but for some reason you are inclined to favor the company that made the lower offer. If the salary it offered had been the same as that offered by the other company, you would have accepted its offer at once. You are obliged to make your decision early next week.

Can you call the low-offer company and say, "I have another offer, 10 percent above yours, and if you'll meet it, I'll come with you." You can—you might even get away with it—but I wouldn't advise such an action. Major companies don't like to be hustled by anyone—and certainly not by about-to-be-graduated students.

If you claim a higher salary offer, are you prepared to support the claim? An unconscionable applicant might manufacture a purported offer out of whole cloth. It would not be improper, since you have broached the matter, for the company to question you on the offer. Who made it, for instance? Are you ready to divulge this information?

Assuming that the company would accept your statement on the other offer, how could you discuss your dilemma without damage to your chances—without issuing an ultimatum?

Could you frame your statement like this?

I have a problem I'd like to discuss with you. I have received an offer from Guaranty Trust for a job similar to the one you offered me. Their offer is $1,500 higher than yours. That makes my decision difficult, as I would really prefer to be with you. Money isn't everything, of course, but in my position it is important to me. Is there anything you can tell me that will help me make my decision?

To me, this appears to be an excellent approach. Our friend doesn't say, "Pay up, or else." He doesn't state that he will refuse the offer if the salary isn't raised, nor does he come out with a direct request for equal salary. He merely asks for a response to his question.

The reply might be:

I can understand your problem, but we have a strict policy on offers, and I'm afraid there is nothing I can do about it.

Our applicant cannot object to such a response. He has been forthright, and so has the other chap. All he can say is that he will have to go back to the drawing board and that he will make his decision known by Monday.

He might even get this answer.

I'm glad you brought this up. I'll be happy to discuss the matter with the policy people, and I'll call you back late tomorrow afternoon.

Much better for our friend.

Let's analyze the original request.

1. The name of the other company was given.
2. The amount of salary differential was stated.
3. No demand for equal pay was made.
4. No ultimatum was issued.
5. The applicant merely asked for help in making his decision.

When the applicant receives his answer, no matter what it is, he will be in a better position to make his final choice.

Hints:

□ If something is on your mind with respect to an offer, don't hesitate to discuss it with the person from whom the offer came.

□ Don't make demands or issue ultimatums.

□ You owe it to yourself and the company as well to explore every avenue open to you.

□ When you hear the company decision, don't argue or try to change it.

□ Accept it, and get back to the mind-making-up process.

Company problems when making offers

Put yourself in the position of a recruiter trying to fill 11 positions in his company—6 in the area of finance and 5 in marketing. He has interviewed more than 100 men and women and has invited 30 of them to office visits. He must schedule these over a period of three weeks as it is not easy to have all his department heads on hand at the same time. More days will be consumed in picking out the individuals to whom offers will be made. Once the offers are mailed out, the applicants are entitled to adequate time in which to make their decisions. A problem in logistics presents itself.

In a smaller company with fewer jobs to offer, the problem is much simpler.

Applicants must be aware of what goes on inside a company when it is trying to fill positions. If you are told, at the conclusion of a plant visit, that you will hear within three weeks, do not be surprised or disappointed if the news does not arrive on the appointed date. As we have suggested, let a couple of days go by and then call to show your continued interest.

You might be given the answer on the spot, or you might

be told that the company needs another week or 10 days before it can make a decision.

What is happening? Suppose the marketing division has picked the top five candidates and made offers to them. Two accept within three days; one rejects the offer; and the other two ask for and are granted additional time to make a decision. The company immediately makes an offer to the next person on the list. Within a week or two it may have to extend additional offers. The longer the company delays its offers, the greater is the risk that they will be declined because other positions have been accepted. As a result companies are as desirous as applicants to complete the hiring process as quickly as possible.

What does all this mean to an applicant who has not been among the recipients of the first round of offers? First of all, he shouldn't panic if the company postpones the notification date. Not every applicant will be picked in the first round. How many rounds are there in the annual professional basketball draft?

Whether we like it or not, we live in and are a part of an elitist system. Some people are more desirable than others— this, too, is a fact of life. Class leaders will always be the most attractive prospects for the top employers. They may receive four or five offers, but they can accept only one. Each job they decline adds one more to the pot to be divided among their classmates.

The process will be repeated in the second round of offers, and even in the third or fourth round. It may take some time for the action to reach mere mortals like you and me. But, when the offer finally comes, it will be an offer of the same job, the same responsibilities and opportunities, and in our hearts we know we can do a job as good as or better than the job that would have been done by the person to whom the offer was originally made.

So, don't be discouraged if companies delay decisions. They are as interested as you in filling the opening.

Hints:

□ Stay in touch. Continue to show desire for and interest in the job. Don't let the company forget you.

□ Don't be discouraged by delays.

Rejections (bullets)

Into every life a little rain must fall. In job hunting the rain takes the form of bullets—notifications that companies will not offer you a job.

Bullets are as familiar to a job hunter as are rejection slips to an aspiring author. Some are well written and try to soften the impact; they'll tell you what a great person you are and how sorry they are, but . . . Others are cold, impersonal.

The first two or three bullets you receive will be a blow to your pride. After that you will begin to view them as a normal occurrence in the hunt cycle. Remember, you can accept only one job, and as long as you get a single adequate offer, you must either reject or be rejected by every other company to which you have applied. Companies, too, are disappointed when they are turned down by an applicant to whom they have tendered an offer.

What do you do when you receive a bullet? Do you tear up the letter and throw out the notes you made on the original interview and the plant trip, if there was one? Perhaps, and perhaps not. If the company didn't turn you on particularly and your interview didn't go very well, you probably decided at the time that the company was unlikely to want to talk with you further. In such a case, tear up the letter and throw away your notes. Good riddance.

Suppose, however, that the interview had, to your belief, gone well and that you were hoping for an invitation to visit the home office of the company. Suppose the bullet came as a surprise and even as a shock. In such a case I would suggest that you review your notes carefully. Check them to see whether you can determine why the interviewer turned you down. Wait a day or two, and then call him. The wait will allow your disappointment to run its course and thus permit you to view the rejection objectively.

Tell the interviewer you are disappointed, and ask him what caused him to feel you should not be considered for the job. Such an action will do two things for you. It will inform the recruiter that you are still interested in the company, and, if he responds openly, it may teach you something about your interviewing technique that you were unaware of. Perhaps you pressed too hard, or conversely, perhaps you were too bland. You may have destroyed your chances by talking too much or too little. There may be a weakness in your résumé which should be corrected. If the recruiter will level with you, his comments can be of inestimable value. Experience is a wonderful teacher, provided we learn from it.

Consider rejection as a normal part of the recruiting process. Profit by your mistakes, and realize that the only way you can do this is to learn what they were. Most recruiters are decent, kindly people and will react favorably to an honest request for help. If a recruiter is of the other type and won't even give you the time of day, be thankful you didn't go to work for his company.

If you receive a bullet after a good first interview and an office visit that you thought went well, don't take the bullet lying down if you really want that specific job with that specific company. I know a young woman who was turned down by an advertising agency three times. She refused to take no for an answer, and finally the agency, perhaps too exhausted to continue the battle, hired her. She was an immediate success on the job. Such tactics work in only a few cases, but in this instance the young woman's persistence and obvious desire for the job impressed the people with whom she came in contact.

A courteous acknowledgment of a rejection is never a mistake, especially if the applicant regards the job and the company highly. Situations do change, and there may be a second chance for the individual who doesn't give up too easily.

Let us suppose you had a good interview with a company high on your list of desirable prospects and you were invited to a further interview at headquarters. Two weeks later you received a bullet—friendly and polite, but still a rejection. You called, and you were told that there was no adverse feeling about you or your credentials—actually, they liked you—but that other candidates were judged to be superior to you. Fair enough.

Why not sit down and write a letter like this?

Dear Mr. Throckmorton:

Thank you for talking to me yesterday. I can understand your position, and I appreciate your kindness in explaining it to me.

I do want you to know that I am still greatly interested in your company and hope that if any other opening occurs, you will keep me in mind.

Sincerely,

Kathy Horton

The letter takes 10 minutes to write and costs about a quarter. It may be time and money wasted; on the other hand, it may lead to a job offer a month from now. Mr. Throckmorton can't help but be impressed by your good manners and your desire to join his company. To mix a metaphor, keep all your irons in the fire and your quiver filled with arrows.

Hints:

☐ Learn to accept bullets as facts of life, not deadly insults.
☐ If you really want a job, keep going after it.
☐ Don't hesitate to ask why you were turned down.
☐ Profit from your experience.
☐ Keep the door open as long as you can.

8

Advice to the experienced job hunter

Up to this point we have been concerned almost entirely with the efforts of soon-to-be-graduated students who are seeking to enter the job market through the campus recruiting process. This avenue is not normally open to individuals who have completed their schooling and have been gainfully employed for a period ranging up to 30 years or even more. Job hunting is a different game for these people, but résumés, letters, and interviews remain an integral part of their efforts.

The résumé

Let us start with a discussion of the résumé prepared by such a person. In the first place he should not attempt to restrict himself to a single page if his achievements require more space for adequate coverage. Furthermore, a revision in format is recommended. It may not even be appropriate to start with a statement of job objective—this important ele-

155

ment may be handled in the cover letter. Also, since recent experience is of paramount importance, the details on education may be compressed and relegated to a later section of the résumé.

It is essential that the résumé begin with a statement of the author's competence in his field. If he is a sales executive, he should outline the areas of sales management of which he is a master. If he is a financial specialist, he should indicate the functions in which he has demonstrated competence, such as budgeting, cost analysis, money management, financial planning, and computer systems.

The author should not force the reader to make his own judgment as to the author's knowledge or experience in a specific area of his profession.

In addition, the résumé should describe briefly the business of the author's present and previous employers if the companies are not well known, and it should state fully his responsibilities and achievements in the jobs he held.

This résumé writer must also give thought to an explanation of why he left a previous job. If his company was absorbed by another company and he became redundant, as the British put it, there is no reason why he should not mention the fact. On the other hand, if he was politely but firmly eased out because he had made egregious mistakes in judgment that cost his employer a few million dollars, he might decide not to mention this depressing fact.

If our executive is employed at present but is dissatisfied with his position and wishes to make a change, he will probably not give his employer's name and he will make sure there is no possibility that his résumé will reach his boss's desk.

We have recommended that persons who are graduating in a few months should say nothing about salary in their résumés. The experienced executive will include information on this subject. It is important that he give evidence of the value of the services he has rendered in the past. If he is applying for a $60,000-a-year job and can claim an income of $50,000 in his last position, he is able to demonstrate his qualification for the opening. Salary is a measure of worth. It is debatable, however, whether this information should be included in the résumé or mentioned in the cover letter that is sent to a prospective employer. I prefer the latter course. Compensation is, after all, a personal matter, and details on compensation should be disclosed only to a single individual in an organization.

Our friend will mention civic activities as well as memberships in professional societies. If he is an author, he will list the titles of books and articles that he has written.

The top-level executive

Enough of these generalizations. Let's pick an executive who is forced to make a job switch, and let's see how he handles the situation. Also, for a change of pace we will choose a person who has achieved marked success over the years. The principles controlling his actions are the same as the ones that apply to a junior executive who finds himself in the same boat. And why shouldn't we enjoy the pleasure of fantasizing about the trials and tribulations of a man who has made it big? After all, we could be in his glossy Guccis in a few years.

John L. Sullivan is our man. He discusses his situation with a friend, Ed Doughman. Several days later Doughman calls to tell him that he has mentioned his name and circumstances to E. J. Blankenship, president of a large company that is looking for a national sales manager to head one of its divisions. Doughman passes along Blankenship's suggestion that Sullivan write him and enclose a résumé.

The letter that Sullivan writes on his personal, not his office, stationery appears on page 159.

And the résumé he encloses with the letter is shown on page 160.

An analysis of what Sullivan included in and excluded from his letter might be helpful.

First of all, he didn't overwhelm Blankenship with a mass of material. His friend, Ed Doughman, must have whetted Blankenship's interest, as Blankenship did ask Sullivan to write him. Doughman opened the door, and now it is Sullivan's job to get his foot in. The purpose of the letter and the résumé is to secure a lunch date with Blankenship. From that time forward Sullivan will be on his own. If his credentials and characteristics fit Universal's needs, his expertise and personality will determine whether he gets the job, provided it interests him.

You will note that Sullivan offered salary information in his letter, not in his résumé. Blankenship might circulate the résumé to other top executives in his organization, but he would probably regard the letter as confidential and keep it in his personal file.

You will also note that Sullivan explained why he wanted a change and made it clear that he was not being replaced because of any failure on his part. In addition, he let Blankenship know that Titan was aware that he was in the market and he made no secret of his situation.

In his résumé Sullivan did not fill two pages outlining his present responsibilities. Blankenship, as president of a large company, would be familiar with the duties of a national sales manager and would not have to be told that Sullivan had the power to hire, fire, or promote managers. Had Sullivan been in a lesser position, it would have been essential for him to list his responsibilities and authorities more completely.

JOHN L. SULLIVAN
1185 Madison Avenue
New York, New York 10022

February 12, 19XX

Mr. E. J. Blankenship, President
Universal Corporation
355 Park Avenue
New York, New York 10022

Dear Mr. Blankenship:

   Ed Doughman suggested I write you concerning your search for a national
sales manager in your consumer products division.

   My present employer, Titan Home Cleaning Equipment Corporation, has
recently been taken over by Conglomerate Industries, and a number of
executives, including me, have been told we will be replaced by men of its
own choice. The company is aware that we are searching for other positions.

   For the year just ended, my base pay, including bonus, amounted to
approximately $150,000 plus generous benefits. I am 54 years old, and I
look forward to another 10 years of productive service.

   A brief résumé covering my career to date is enclosed.

   Early next month I will start an extended sales promotion trip through the
country, but until then I plan to be in New York. I would appreciate an
opportunity to meet you and discuss our mutual needs.

                              Yours truly,

                              John L. Sullivan

                              John L. Sullivan
                              Tel.: 350-4388

JOHN L. SULLIVAN
1185 Madison Avenue
New York, New York 10022
Telephone: (212) 350-4388

Demonstrated success in all areas of direct marketing of tangible property to ultimate consumer. Experienced in:

1. Personal selling
2. Branch management
3. Division and regional management
4. Control of national selling organization
5. Hiring and motivating salesmen and managers
6. Development and introduction of new products
7. Planning and conducting meetings and conventions
8. Preparing and controlling budgets and quotas

EXPERIENCE   **19XX to present**
Titan Home Cleaning Equipment Corporation, Vice President, Sales. Responsible for production of 6,000 commission salesmen assigned to 246 branches throughout continental United States. Six Regional Managers under personal supervision. They work through 24 Division Managers, each responsible for approximately 10 branches.

Since assumption of present position, have doubled the number of branches and quadrupled annual sales.

19XX to 19XX
Same company. Started as salesman in Pittsburgh. Appointed Branch Manager, Harrisburg, in 19XX; Division Manager, Louisville, in 19XX; Regional Manager, Dallas, in 19XX.

19XX to 19XX
Salesman for Standard-Vacuum Corporation. Sold heating oil to commercial users. Fuller Brush salesman and group leader—one year.

EDUCATION   Penn State University, BS Engineering, 19XX

OUTSIDE   Member, Mayor's Committee on Interracial Relations. Director,
ACTIVITIES   Boys' Club of New York. Vice Chairman, Community Services Association of New York. Director, Stuyvesant Savings Bank. Member and former president of National Sales Executives Association.

PUBLICATIONS   Author of *Successful Direct Selling* (New York: Caravelle Books, 19XX). Frequent contributor to *Sales Executives Magazine*.

CLUBS   University Club of New York
Westchester Country Club, Harrison, New York
Farmington Country Club, Charlottesville, Virginia

Sullivan spent little time on his education and the jobs he held early in his career, but he did report his outside activities and publications in detail. These sections of his résumé reveal him to be a civic-minded individual with distinguished accomplishments and a recognized authority in his field. Contrary to popular belief, reputable publishers are usually exceedingly selective in accepting manuscripts for publication.

Sullivan makes no mention of references. If Blankenship wishes to check his character, he can solicit the necessary information from the clubs and organizations whose names he has been given.

The junior executive

Not all job switchers inhabit an aerie as lofty as Sullivan's. We will assume that you have spent the five years since your graduation from college with a savings and loan association. Your progress has been excellent, but your husband has been offered a substantial promotion which will require you to move to New York. You want to find a job there, and you have decided that your best opportunity will be in the field of commercial banking. Unfortunately, you know no one in any of the major banks, but annual reports are available to you, and from them you pick out the names of the vice presidents who head what the banks call their human resources departments. You write to three men, enclosing a résumé, and await results. You have deliberately kept the number of applications low on your first round so that if you find that there is a weakness in either your letter or your résumé, you won't have blown all your chances in one fell swoop. The letter you write on your own stationery is shown on page 162.

A copy of Marsha's résumé is shown on page 163.

MARSHA FISK
12 Revere Lane
Richmond, Virginia 22611

October 16, 19XX

Mr. George Bagley, Vice President
Netherlands Trust Company
380 Park Avenue
New York, New York 10022

Dear Mr. Bagley:

I would like to secure a position in your bank. My husband is being transferred to New York, and I have notified my employer, Piedmont Savings and Loan Association, that we are moving the first of next month.

I believe that my five years' experience in banking will make me a valuable employee for you, as I am familiar with teller operations, customer relations, new account solicitation, and mortgage loan application procedures.

Please let me know if I may call on you about three weeks from now.

Sincerely,

Marsha Fisk

Marsha Fisk

Résumé enclosed.

MARSHA FISK
12 Revere Lane
Richmond, Virginia 22611
Telephone: (804) 200-4183

EMPLOYMENT OBJECTIVE	Seek position in commercial banking as a lending officer or in solicitation of new business.

EXPERIENCE

June 19XX to present
Piedmont Savings and Loan Association, Richmond, Virginia. Loan officer with responsibility for taking loan applications from home buyers, scheduling appraisals, confirming employment and credit information, analyzing financial statements, preparing and making presentations to the Loan Committee.

July 19XX to June 19XX
Same employer. New Accounts Manager. Aided customers in choosing which type of account was most advantageous to them and prepared forms for signature. Spent two days a week soliciting Payroll Deduction Accounts from local employers. In 11 months signed up 14 companies, with more than 1,200 individual accounts opened.

September 19XX to July 19XX
Same employer. Worked as teller and learned all operations of computer terminal. For last six months worked one-half time in bookkeeping department and became familiar with accounting procedures on balance sheet and profit and loss statements.

EDUCATION

University of North Carolina, AB, 19XX. Major in English with several courses in microeconomics, macroeconomics, marketing, and finance. While at Piedmont S&L received certificate for completion of seven U.S. Savings and Loan League courses in consumer credit, business law, accounting, human relations, and so forth.

PERSONAL

Married, no children. Husband with R. J. Reynolds Corporation for seven years, at present as field sales manager. We are both interested in tennis and skiing, art, and modern music.

REFERENCES

Will be furnished on request.

What has Marsha attempted to accomplish with her letter
and résumé, and how well has she succeeded?

The letter

It is addressed personally to the vice president in charge of
hiring and personnel. "Dear Mr. Bagley" is much better than
"Dear Sir."

The letter is short and sweet, yet see how much information it contains.

1. Marsha wants a job.
2. At present she is employed in a financial institution.
3. She and her husband are moving to New York, and she
   establishes the date of the move and of her availability
   for an interview.
4. She has five years' experience, and she has worked in four
   specified areas.
5. She asks permission to call Mr. Bagley when she arrives in
   New York.

What else is there to say? The résumé supplies specifics on
Marsha's objective, experience, and education that are not
contained in the letter.

The résumé

It starts with a statement of job objective that is compatible with Marsha's previous experience and relates to areas of
paramount importance to the prospective employer.

Marsha lists her three positions in the savings and loan
association—the most recent one first. She not only identifies
the job but also outlines its responsibilities, and when she has
an opportunity to brag, she accepts it and states her accomplishments.

A reader should be impressed by the progress Marsha has shown, and the wide exposure she has had to the business of her employer is evidence of her motivation and desire to succeed.

The section on education is compact, but it lists study areas and mentions the special courses Marsha has taken that help her to understand the business of her employer.

The personal section, too, is short. It indicates, however, that the marriage is a close one between two individuals of similar tastes and interests.

I don't think Marsha will have much difficulty in finding the job she wants in New York.

Hints:

- Adapt the cover letter to the circumstances of your entrée to the opportunity.
- Keep it short and to the point.
- Disclose your reason for leaving your previous job if it is not discreditable to you.
- Be sure to let addressee know whether your present employer is aware that you are looking for another position.
- If you wish your application to be considered confidential, say so.
- State the name of your present employer unless there is good reason not to.
- The letter is the door opener for the résumé, and the purpose of the résumé is to secure an interview for you.
- If necessary, explain the business of your previous employers. Describe your job responsibilities and authorities.
- If your accomplishments have been noteworthy, don't be reluctant to mention them, but don't be a braggart.
- If you have extensive work experience, you should concentrate on that rather than the details of your education. How

you employ what you have learned is more important than what you were taught at school.

- [ ] If you have earned in excess of $30,000 a year, it might be wise to make this known to a prospective employer in a confidential cover letter.
- [ ] If you are a junior executive, salary requirements may be discussed at a later date.

9

Other approaches for job hunters

It is unfortunate that not all desirable potential employers recruit at your school or college. New York banks may not visit campuses in Arkansas, and computer firms based in Houston may not send representatives to Connecticut. Smaller companies may recruit only at institutions within a hundred miles of their home offices even though they hire a dozen graduates a year. If a recruiter does visit your school, you may not be able to secure a place on his schedule or a conflict may make it impossible for you to meet him.

Consequently, you may be forced to find another avenue to present your qualifications to a preferred employer, and many are open to the job hunter. Among the avenues often used by the soon-to-be-graduates are direct mail campaigns, employment agencies, help wanted ads, family, and friends. Executive career consultants (headhunters) and personal agents are usually retained only by experienced executives with impressive performance records.

167

Direct mail

There is nothing arcane or esoteric about this approach. All one requires is a list of companies, a letter, a copy of a résumé, and a roll of stamps of the proper denomination. It is no problem to dust off the trusty Underwood, type out the body of a letter, run off a hundred copies, fill in company names and addresses, and send the letters along with a résumé to a hundred "Dear Sirs."

Such an effort will probably result in the receipt of 50 form letter responses advising you that your résumé has been placed in the appropriate file. It is not stated that this storage receptacle is usually circular in shape and metallic in fabrication and is customarily emptied each evening. Yet, a mail campaign can be effective if it is properly planned and carried out. The following steps are recommended.

1. Choose your targets. Do your research in the library. Presumably, you have already decided what industries appeal to you and what type of job you want in them. Dig out the names of the leading companies in the field.
2. Study the companies—read annual reports and analyze financial data.
3. Ferret out the name of the individual who heads the personnel or human resources department. You might even have to make a phone call to get the name and title right, but it will be a dollar well spent.
4. Compose and write your cover letters—an individual one for each company. No copies or reproductions. Your letters must be professional in both appearance and content.
5. Mail the letters along with a copy of your résumé.
6. Then, sit back and await responses.

The right cover letter is not easy to compose. We have already read what John L. Sullivan and Marsha Fisk have written. Both of them were looking for a new job, but their situation is different from yours. Unlike you, they have had business experience and they are employed at present.

What information should your cover letter include? No problem here. It should state:

1. Your present status—student about to be graduated.
2. Your reason for writing—you want a job. Say so. Also, let the reader know what kind of job you want and your qualifications for it.
3. Why you are writing that particular company—you must have a reason. What is it?
4. What you can contribute to the company.
5. Your availability for an interview—time and place.
6. A request for a reply.

John Ball, a senior at a western college, is seeking a job with a chemical company on the eastern seaboard. Unfortunately, none of the companies of John's choice recruit at his institution. After completing his research, John writes the first draft of his cover letter.

Dear Mr. Glencannon:

I am a student at Jackson College majoring in chemistry and am interested in the possibility of securing employment with your company.

I rank in the top 10 percent of my class, and my specialty has been inorganic chemistry.

I would like to secure employment with one of the leading chemical companies, and your corporation is certainly in the top rank.

I am enclosing a copy of my résumé, and I would appreciate the opportunity to discuss my application with you.

Sincerely,

John Ball

If we are charitable, we can say that this letter has one virtue—it is short. Otherwise, it has very little to recommend it. Among its faults are:

1. Every paragraph begins with "I."
2. John should not be interested in the *possibility* of a job; he wants *a job.*
3. In the second paragraph there is little relationship between class rank and major area of study. Rewriting is necessary.
4. The next paragraph is weak. It flatters the company and accomplishes nothing else.
5. Of course, John wants an interview. How will it be arranged? Does he expect the company to send one of its executive jets to pick him up and fly him to Wilmington?
6. The writing style is poor. Editing is required.

John agrees with our assessment when he reads what he has written. With freshly sharpened pencil he goes back to the drawing board, and the letter on page 171 is his revised version, written on school stationery.

He has said it all, hasn't he? Status, what he wants, qualifications, ability to contribute, availability, and a request for an answer. What more is needed?

A master's candidate with several years of full-time employment behind him will use three or four lines of his cover letter to relate his previous experience to the type of job he is seeking.

Hints:

□ Cover letters should be brief.
□ Tell the man who you are, what you want, why he should give it to you, and when you will be able to make your pitch to him.

JACKSON COLLEGE
Jackson, Montana

April 16, 19XX

Mr. Colin Glencannon, Vice President
Human Resources Department
Amalgamated Chemical Corporation
Wilmington, Delaware 07536

Dear Mr. Glencannon:

I will graduate in May from Jackson College with a degree in chemistry.

It is my desire to secure a job with a leading chemical company with a wide range of products. My training, especially in inorganic chemistry, and my summer experiences in selling positions convince me that I can make a contribution to your company as a sales engineer selling chemicals to commercial users.

Soon after graduation I plan to visit relatives in Philadelphia and I could call at your office at any time between June 8 and June 20. Please let me know whether you can arrange an interview with me during that period.

Sincerely,

John Ball

John Ball
17 Oak Lane
Jackson, Montana 12620

Résumé enclosed.

- ☐ Don't mention salary desired.
- ☐ Don't expect the company to pay your travel expenses to the interview.
- ☐ Avoid too many personal pronouns, but don't eliminate them entirely. You are talking about yourself.
- ☐ No matter how many letters you write, have each one typed individually.
- ☐ Smoke out the name and title of each addressee.

As a complement to the interviewing process on campus, I strongly recommend the use of direct mail application to all men and women entering the job market. If you are interested in the banking field, it would be foolish and unrealistic to assume that all the most prestigious financial institutions will recruit at your school. Why deny yourself the opportunity of securing employment with a company just because it did not have the foresight to send a representative to interview you. Keep all your options open—don't fence yourself in.

Employment agencies

These organizations provide a worthwhile and needed service. If an applicant lives in a large metropolitan area, they can be of great help to him in finding employment. It is doubtful, however, whether Laurel, Mississippi, can boast of an employment agency with clients offering jobs in Chicago, San Francisco, New York, or even Phoenix.

A corporation employs an employment agency to screen job candidates for it. Job descriptions for open positions are given to the agency, which attempts to pick likely candidates from the applications it has on file. If necessary, it will advertise the job in local newspapers to attract more applicants.

A job hunter visits an agency, undergoes a screening interview, fills out an agency application form, and then waits for a call when an appropriate opening is available. At that time the applicant is given a briefing session at the agency and is sent to the company for an interview. In some cases the decision of whom to send is left to the agency, and in other cases the company checks copies of applications received from the agency and designates the individuals it desires to interview.

The agency usually collects its fee from the employer, not the applicant, but in some instances the applicant will be required to pay part or all of the fee should he be given the job.

If no job suitable to his talents is available at the moment, a job hunter in his initial discussion with an agency will have only one subject to talk about—his desirability as an employee if the right opportunity presents itself from a client of the agency.

It will be up to the applicant to sell himself to the agency interviewer. Appearance, manners, and ability to express himself are vitally important. So is the applicant's ability to display his motivation, intelligence, and capability in their best light.

The applicant will know what he wants to do and will convince the interviewer that he has the ability to live up to his claims about himself.

If the agency has an opening for which the applicant is fitted, additional demands will be made of him. Once the position is described, it will be the applicant's responsibility to show his fitness to handle it. The company will have made clear to the agency what characteristics it is looking for in an applicant, and the interviewer, through a series of questions, will attempt to discover whether the applicant meets the desired criteria. This part of the interview will closely parallel a recruiting interview on campus.

The applicant, however, will not yet know what company is offering the job. He is therefore relieved of the responsibility to be familiar with the company's operations, but the situation will be difficult for him to handle since he must speak in general rather than specific terms about his skills.

No matter what the circumstances of the agency interview are, the applicant will have at least two copies of his résumé available. At the conclusion of the meeting he will probably be asked to fill out an agency application form which is nothing but a rehash of his own résumé in a different format.

When an agency sends an applicant to a company, the applicant can expect the same kind of initial interview that he would have with a recruiter on campus. He should use the same techniques he has learned previously. Quite often the hiring process is speeded up when a company engages an agency to assist it in its hiring process.

The screening interview and the office visit interviews may be compressed into a single session, and an offer or a rejection may be forthcoming at the end. The lower the job level, the higher will be the probability of a quick answer.

There is no reason why an applicant should not register with a number of employment agencies. Each has its own corporate clients, and the more complete the job hunter's coverage of the job market, the more opportunities will be available to him.

Hints:

□ Register with several agencies.

□ Don't let distance scare you off. If the closest large metropolitan area if 50 miles away, spend a couple of days there getting listed with a half-dozen agencies. The more the merrier. If a suitable opening occurs, they'll be glad to spend a dollar on a phone call to earn a handsome fee.

□ Use employment agencies, but use them right.

□ Draw on your campus interviewing skills when applying to an employment agency.

□ When an agency secures a company interview for you and reveals the company's name, do your homework before you show up for your interview.

Help wanted ads

The classified and financial sections of nearly all newspapers contain advertisements of positions available. These advertisements will include a job description, some indication of salary, and perhaps a mention of the incentives and benefits offered by the company. The name of the company is not always given, but if not, its size and character are usually stated. Applicants are asked to call or write. If you write, you are requested to enclose a résumé, and almost all advertisements specify that you submit your salary history. Usually, you are assured that replies will be considered in confidence.

An ad in *The Wall Street Journal* or the *New York Times* financial section costs a lot of money. The jobs offered in these publications are, for the most part, well-paying ones with salaries ranging up to hundreds of thousands of dollars. A single ad insertion may bring replies numbering in the thousands.

Answer a few ads. The odds against you are great, but so is the reward if you are successful. A toll-free call costs you nothing, and the expense of a letter accompanied by a résumé is no big deal. If you are encouraged by the reaction of advertisers, keep at it.

Let's look at a representative ad in *The Wall Stree Journal.*

PERSONNEL SPECIALIST

A fast-growing billion-dollar service-oriented New York company needs to add a Personnel Specialist to its corporate staff.

A minimum of three years' experience and an advanced degree are required. Knowledge of Benefits, Compensation, Employee Relations, and Training is essential. Salary open—20K base.

If you are interested in a rapidly expanding opportunity, submit your résumé and salary history in confidence to:

Box Ez 8P16, The Wall Street Journal

An equal opportunity employer M/F

A response might read like the example on page 177.

James J. has done himself proud. In a short letter he has covered every base, shown how he meets all the criteria established by Box Ez 8P16, and in addition told why he is seeking a change in scenery. His résumé will give further details about his present job and the business of Listex corporation and will cover other personal details.

Since it would be unwise for James J. to receive mail or phone calls at the office, he has supplied his home address and phone number.

I wouldn't be surprised if James J. hears from Box Ez 8P16 in a few days.

Hints:

□ Again—keep it short and to the point.

□ In the letter, demonstrate your qualifications to meet job specifications.

□ Don't be reluctant to state your reasons for wanting to make a change—provided they are not to your discredit.

□ Ask for confidential treatment of your application if this is desirable.

□ Be realistic. If you earn $20,000 on your present job, don't answer an ad for a $100,000 position. You won't get it.

September 18, 19XX

Box Ez 8P16
The Wall Street Journal
22 Cortlandt Street
New York, New York 10007

Subject: Your ad WSJ 9/16/19XX

Dear Sir:

I have been engaged in personnel work for the past four years with the Listex Corporation of Elizabeth, New Jersey. At present I am assistant to the Vice President—Human Resources and my base pay is $19,000 a year.

My experience covers all the areas you mention, and in addition I have participated in contract negotiations with our union on several occasions.

I received a BA from Columbia in 19XX, and I expect to be awarded an MBA from NYU next January.

It is my intention to make a career of personnel work, and I wish to make a change because my superior is only a few years older than I am and there is little opportunity for advancement in my present position. Please regard this information as confidential.

The enclosed résumé will give details of my experience and background.

I will appreciate an opportunity to discuss my application with you at your convenience.

Sincerely,

James J. Corbett
12 Garden Court
Elizabeth, New Jersey 07840
Home phone: (201) 572-0001

Friends and family as sources of leads

Don't ignore this avenue—it might be very productive. If the circumstances make it inadviseable for you to tell your present employer that you are desirous of a change, discretion is advised in acquainting people of your intentions. Unless controlled, news has a nasty habit of reaching places it shouldn't. So, if you are employed and don't want your company to know you are looking for another job, don't broadcast your intentions to the world. Mention the fact only to the individuals whose discretion you can trust.

On the other hand, if you are between jobs, let the world know it, especially if your unemployed status has resulted from no fault of your own. There is no stigma attached to being out of a job these days. Swallow your pride, and use any possible assistance available to you to help you find another.

Business acquaintances as well as friends can and will help you. So will uncles, aunts, in-laws, cousins.

Hints:

- Utilize all your resources.
- Pick your confidants carefully if discretion is necessary.

I have been thinking about the first of these hints. *Utilize all your resources*—that makes a lot of sense to me. Go through the recruiting process; write letters; list yourself with employment agencies; solicit the assistance of faculty, the placement office, friends, family members. If you have been employed, use business connections and fellow members of professional organizations to smoke out opportunities for you. Saturation techniques work.

As I write this, I am reminded of an incident that occurred many years ago when I was working in New York. I had become acquainted with a chap, a few years younger than I, who was a member of a society to which I belonged. He worked in the financial department of a medium-size privately owned company, and when the treasurer retired, he expected, with good reason, to be promoted to fill the opening. To his dismay the position was given to the president's inexperienced and unqualified son-in-law. My friend promptly resigned and organized a job hunting campaign. He registered with a number of employment agencies, answered advertisements, wrote letters, and enlisted the aid of everyone he knew. Each morning at opening time he ensconced himself at a table in the main reading room of the New York Public Library, just across the street from my office on Forty-second Street. In his chosen spot he researched details on the corporations he was writing and checked all the papers to discover employment opportunities that interested him.

The country was then experiencing a periodic recession, and Bobby's results were disappointing even though he was approaching his task with professional expertise.

One morning as I read the *Times* on my commuting train from Darien, I noticed the obituary of a relatively young man I had known slightly as the assistant to the treasurer of a large corporation. His boss was a good friend, and I called him as soon as I reached my office. He expressed shock at the sudden death of his assistant and then mentioned that he was deeply concerned about replacing him—there was no one in his department qualified to assume his duties.

I told him to relax; I would have an exceptionally competent replacement in his office within an hour. My secretary scurried across the street, returning with Bobby in tow, and I sent him uptown after a short briefing. Bobby returned late that afternoon, shook my hand, and said he was starting work the next morning.

He stayed with the company until he retired, and each

Christmas I receive a card from him. The earlier cards contained a picture of Bobby and his wife and their ever-increasing number of children, but now I find it difficult to count the family—five children and a dozen or more grandchildren.

The moral is: Utilize all your resources—you never know when or where lightening will strike.

The value of a summer job and how to get one

For a college or graduate school student good summer jobs are as scarce as hen's teeth. It's a damn shame, but there it is.

Money is not the prime consideration. Digging ditches in Sioux City may pay better than being an intern with Union Carbide, but a perceptive individual might conclude that the opportunities offered by a 10-foot hole in Iowa are inferior to those that could develop from an office job with a top-quality corporation in New York.

A number of the better companies do hire students for summer work. They have learned that a well-managed summer program will achieve two objectives for them: it will enable them to complete annoying special projects in an acceptable fashion, and, even more important, it will enable them to make a valid judgment on the desirability of offering a permanent job to a summer worker after his graduation.

Students find these assignments rewarding. Working in a marketing program for General Mills is—to use another word I despise—more "meaningful" than the usual run of summer jobs. A relatively inexperienced individual can observe how a large well-run company operates. If he is enrolled in a graduate school, he can see the use and value of the techniques he has studied and he can decide from personal experience whether or not he would like to work for that company if his performance during the summer earns him an offer of a permanent job.

How does a student go about securing such a plum? Recruiters for companies that have summer programs may arrange to have a list of openings posted on a school bulletin board and may allocate interviewers a block of time for non-graduating students. Other, more enlightened organizations appoint a summer-job-only recruiter who operates like any other recruiter. College juniors and first-year students in graduate schools will prepare for interviews as if they were graduating. They will do their homework on companies, prepare résumés, and develop and practice their interviewing technique. They will also engage in a letter campaign directed at companies that do not recruit, in the manner described earlier in this chapter. They will not be as selective in their choice of targets as a soon-to-be-graduate would be, because their main desire is to get a summer job, and for that purpose Bankers Trust is just as good as Ma Bell or ITT.

Many placement offices do not do all they should for non-graduating students even though they have an equal obligation to these students. During the off-season placement offices should be out beating the bushes in an effort to expand the number of organizations recruiting at their institution. In doing so, they should not neglect to point out the advantage of offering summer work to worthy students. It's an educational process all around. Placement offices must be made aware of their responsibilities, and employers must realize the value to them of summer programs.

Understandably, companies offering summer work seldom, if ever, arrange office visits except when the travel distance is minimal. A company representative who recruits for summer work will turn over the résumés he has collected and his interview notes to the person who is offering the position, and that person makes his decision and writes the lucky applicant.

I would suggest that a student who wishes to secure a summer job start his campaign well before the opening of the regular recruiting season. If he does so, he will be able, in the application letter he writes the company, to refer to the fact that recruiters for permanent jobs will be interviewing on certain dates and that he would appreciate an opportunity to talk with one of them. Don't wait to write your letter until after the recruiters have come and gone.

If the company does not recruit at the college or graduate school, a student must depend on the quality of his letter and his résumé to secure a summer job for him. He may also plan a short trip during Christmas vacation or spring break to a metropolitan area where he can call on prospective employers. He should write, enclosing a copy of his résumé, and ask for an interview.

Securing a summer job with a prestigious company is not easy, but the rewards of success can be great. The odds are high that successful completion of a summer assignment will lead to an offer of a permanent job following graduation. Having a firm offer in hand before you start your last school year will give you a warm and comfortable feeling.

Hints:

☐ Keep after your placement office to improve its service to students not about to graduate.

☐ Start sending your letters by the first of December.

☐ Spend as much time on your résumé as you would if you were graduating the following spring.

☐ Do your homework—practice your interviewing technique.

☐ Plan multipurpose interviewing trips whenever time is available and finances permit.

☐ Keep plugging. It's a tough assignment, but the rewards will make it worthwhile.

Conclusion

Well, there you are. I've done the best I can for you, and I sincerely hope that, having read what I have had to say, you are better equipped to make the change from paying for an education to earning a living.

Most of us, for better or worse, have to work to support ourselves, and we realize that the quality of our work will determine the quality of our lifestyle. If we ultimately find the right niche for ourselves, we will enjoy a more productive and satisfying existence. I hope you will agree that work should not be regarded as an end in itself but rather as a means to achieve much more worthy objectives. I have my own belief of what those objectives should be, and I trust that you have developed an awareness of what you hope to accomplish with your life. Think of this, please. There are career objectives, and they are important—no one disputes that—but let us not forget that there are life objectives as well.

Good luck, and my very best wishes to you.

W.G. Ryckman